Juggle and Hide
a memoir

Sharon van Ivan

For my darling Charles, the bravest person I have ever known.

PROLOGUE

Sweet Dreams Are Made Of This?

End of the world.
    I look around and see nothing.
    The destruction is complete. No life of any kind. No flowers. No trees. No people. Nothing is left, nothing at all. I stand alone in the middle of this catastrophe. Dry dirt on a flat plain. A barren desert with no oasis.
    But where is everyone else? Why am I here alone?
    I look down at my dirty bare feet and try to brush off some of the grayish dust that covers my torn gray cotton dress. What color was it before this happened? I can't even remember. Ashes. I am covered with ashes. Ashes in my hair, my eyes, my mouth.
    I am not afraid, merely stunned.
    Then I hear voices in the distance. Wailing. Crying. Begging echoes of pain and deep sorrow. Disaster. Dying. Death.
    The voices grow louder and become one.
    I run toward the sound; hoping it is human. My feet disturb the dust as I move, so I slow my pace to a walk as the voices invade my soul.
    Savemesavemesavemesavemesavemesaveme.
    I stop abruptly at the edge of a deep hole in the earth. I look into the pit without getting close enough to fall in. You are all there in that pit. All of the people on earth are in this one deep, dark canyon of suffering. All of you crammed together, arms reaching upward toward the clear blue sky. Faces covered with ashes show the fear forcing its way through to me. I watch the scene below in utter despair.
    Little girl. Step away from the edge of the pit.
    A booming voice from far above speaks to me. I see no one, but the voice I hear is powerful yet somehow comforting and even loving. I step back. All of your voices are directed toward me.
    Little girl. Step back.
    I obey.
    I want you to help me.

The voice is all encompassing and soothes me again, takes my fears away. It is the only voice I hear now.

I want to begin again. I shall point out the ones I want and need: the good ones, the ones with the strength and the knowledge to rebuild my earth, to rebuild it and make it the utopia I meant for it to be. Now, go over to the edge and look into that hellish pit—not too close.

Carefully, slowly, I look into the deep hole of humbled humanity.

There, over there, see the woman with the glow around her. I want her. She is a scientist. You will save her first. I will choose the rest—one at a time.

I am afraid to ask how I am to manage this.

Stand still and the ones with the white glow around them will come to you. Just reach out. I will give you the strength to save them.

I look around.

Just look at the ones that I light for you. Not the others.

I see my mother clawing her way to the edge of the pit near the spot where I am standing.

My baby, save me.

The voice booms. *No. No. No.*

I cannot bear to see my mother suffer and I instinctively reach out to her. She clutches my hand and as I try to pull her out, she is too heavy for me and pulls me into the pit.

You foolish child.

I look up at the radiant blue sky from deep within the pit and I cry. I know I will never hear that voice again.

I wake up alone in my grandmother's featherbed in the cluttered bedroom of her tiny house on Bittaker Street in Akron, Ohio.

For the first time in my life I know what I want.

I want to die.

I am seven.

Part I

Chapter 1

Mommy's Home

I cannot remember a time when I was not my mother's keeper.

I stare at the back of my mother's head. I sit on her bed. I look over her shoulder and see in the three-sided dressing table mirror that her face is slightly puffy from having her teeth pulled earlier in the day... all of them... and insisting the hack dentist fit the dentures over her raw gums.
"Reach in there and get me my lipstick."
I dig around in her navy blue leather purse, find a shiny black tube and hold it out to her.
"Revlon. Persian Melon."
When she reaches for it, I see how beautiful her nails are. Also, Persian Melon.
She slathers the orangish-red lipstick on, under and over her swollen lips and then smacks her lips together.
"You are damned lucky. You got your father's lips. Get me a Kleenex."
I hand one to her and she gently blots her puckered lips. I continue to gaze at the back of her head while she finishes putting on her going-out-tonight face.
"Get my shoes. And don't ask which ones."
A bit of rummaging in her overflowing closet and I find the new navy blue sling-back pumps she bought to match the dress she is wearing tonight. She slips the shoes on, stands up and looks at herself for a long time in the distorting full-length mirror on the wall next to her closet.
"You're beautiful, Mommy."
"I make myself beautiful. See how everything matches. shoes, purse, dress, everything. Blue. Promise me you will never, never buy cheap makeup."
And without looking at me, she hisses, "Stop biting your nails or you won't ever get a husband. Do I have any lipstick on my teeth?"
She bares her new false teeth in sort of a smile.

I shake my head. She looks like a movie star. I wish I had long curly auburn hair and creamy white skin. My hair is straight and dirty blonde like my father's.

On the way to the front door, she reminds me to not ask her again what time she will come home.

"I lost my keys. You'll have to let me in."

Then she is gone.

The sweet smell of *Arpege* cologne or toilet water or perfume—it annoys her that I never knew which is which— is all that is left of her.

I clean up her getting-ready-to-go-out mess.

Afterward I go to bed fully clothed not knowing whom she might bring home or whether I will even hear her when she bangs on the door. I pray aloud to someone—to anyone—to keep her safe.

At three a.m., I walk the two long blocks to Pete's.

I stand outside for a few minutes beneath the neon sign flashing "Pete's View Lunch." There is no view. There is no window. And I don't think they serve lunch. The door is propped open with an old brown wooden chair.

Taking a deep breath and walking into the crowded bar, with the sickening smell of stale beer, cigarettes and misplaced rage all around me, I search for Pete.

Pete spots me right away.

Pete has no teeth. Not even one.

"Looking for Mommy?"

I nod.

He winks at me and points with his middle finger toward the back. I want to ask him why he has no index fingers, but my mind is on finding my mother.

I push my way through the drunks to the back of the dark narrow room to the bathroom.

Ladies.

I open the door and there she is lying face down on the filthy floor, near the once white toilet.

She has on one navy blue shoe, but her purse is gone. I roll her over with some difficulty and see that the Persian Melon is all but gone, too.

I wet my hands in the disgusting sink and splash cold water on her face.

"What the hell are you doing here, you goddamn little spy? Always watching me."

In an attempt to sit up, she bangs her head on the empty toilet paper holder.

Pete knocks on the door.

"You girls decent?"

He sticks his head in and holds the door open.

"She was in rare form tonight. Caused a real stink with Carney Wells and Crazy Marie."

I flinch. Crazy Marie is my grandmother. My mother's mother. I have to call her Mom instead of Grandma because she says she's too young to be a grandmother.

"Come on. Mommy, let's go home."

"Leave me alone. What are you doing here anyway?"

Then she sees Pete.

"Pete, honey, get me a Seven and Seven."

Pete looks at me and winks again.

"You've had your last drink for tonight. I called you and your kid a cab."

Pete and I pull, push, and shove her into the yellow City Cab. He gives the driver our address on Jewett Street and a couple of dollars.

"Thank you, Pete."

He leans into the cab and gives me a sloppy wet kiss.

On the way home, my mother puts her head in my lap and curses me over and over again for ruining her night, her life.

At our place, I ask the driver to please help me get my mother inside. He is a nice guy. He helps me.

Once inside, she wrenches herself away from us and stumbles and lands on the couch.

The cab driver looks at me like I'm a sideshow freak.

"What are you about six years old?"

"Eight."

I quickly lock the door after he leaves.

Then I hear my baby brother cry out from his crib in my bedroom.

"It's okay, Bobby. Go to sleep now. Mommy's home. Mommy's home."

Chapter 2

The Shiek

Shiekie, my dad, the blonde, blue-eyed, Jewish boy from Brooklyn who taught me how to write my name backwards when I was three, gave me a Remington portable typewriter when I was four, a Brownie Hawkeye Camera when I was five, and took me to my first subtitled film when I was six is also a con artist, card shark, saxophone player, singer, tap dancer, liar, thief, bookie, handicapper, compulsive gambler, pimp, cheat, defender of losers. On this day in 1954, he is a part-time bartender at the Beacon Hotel Bar on the southeast corner of Broadway and 75th in the neighborhood known as Needle Park.

It is summer in Manhattan and I am meeting him at the end of his shift to ride home to Brighton Beach on the D Train, one stop before Coney Island, the end of the line.

I stand across the street from the Beacon. It takes me a while to build up the courage to cross the street and go into the bar. Usually the place is packed, but through the front window I see that there is only one customer this afternoon. Relief wells up inside me as I take the long walk across Broadway.

From all that way, I can see how handsome my father is in his white bartender's jacket, white shirt and black tie. Finally he sees me and waves. I wave back and smile. He keeps waving and I keep waving and then I realize he is waving at a man walking behind me. I stop and let him pass. It's Harry Belafonte. Harry is waving to my dad and laughing. Harry passes me, bangs on the window of the bar and keeps on going.

All right, I do this all the time, I can do this today. I take in the cool dark dampness of the bar as Dinah Washington's voice fills the large room with *What a Difference a Day Makes*.

My dad finally notices me, reaches under the bar, and turns Dinah down.

"Sharon, baby, you know what I like about me? Everything!"

His laugh is infectious, his smile looks genuine, his teeth are capped and to me he is a star. But still I laugh self-consciously as I climb up on my usual stool at the end of the bar. Dad likes me to sit there so I can watch his technique at the cash register. He robs the owner blind. Dad enjoys teaching me the skill of reading the register tape—in the mirror behind the cash register—upside down and backwards.

"Isn't she a little young for even you, Shiekie?"

"Behave yourself, Marco. This is my daughter."

The ageless guy at the other end of the bar moves a few stools closer to me. Trust-fund Marco (Dad calls him that) dresses casually but expensively. It doesn't help. I've met Marco before, but he never remembers me.

"What do you like, honey? I can get you anything you want."

"Go on, Sha, tell him what you like."

I would like to run like hell out of this place is what I would like, but I mumble something about tennis.

"What, honey?"

Marco moves closer.

I freeze up, but force out the words.

"I think I want to learn to play tennis."

They both laugh at me for a long time before Marco puts on his cap and leaves. The Beacon bar is his second home.

Dinah sings quietly in the background, but now the place is empty. Just Dad and me. He leans across the bar and plants a wet kiss on my lips. He always kisses everybody on the lips. A little sloppy but nice because I love him.

This morning he hinted that he has something to tell me, so I wait for whatever the news is this time.

"Sha, remember when I met Betty in Miami?"

I don't really remember when or where he met my stepmother, Betty.

"Sharon, remember she was what seven months pregnant? She went ahead and had this baby, so the doc and I fixed up a death certificate for it for Betty and a birth certificate for the new parents and we let this nice Jewish couple adopt it."

I close my eyes; hold my breath. This is not a joke. This is one of the true stories. I am his confessional. I do not know why. Maybe because I am so quiet that he knows I will never repeat a word of it. I hate that he has to tell me the things he does. I save them all in a part of me that never dies.

"We never told Betty, Sha. Got my own kid."

He takes my hands in his and gives me his knockout smile.

I swallow. I cannot smile this time.

"You all right? This'll fix you right up. Blackberry Brandy."

There is more to his horror story.

"Now, here's this good-looking kid comes up to me on the street the other day and tells me I'm his father. Of all the rotten luck. Wouldn't you know my name was on the birth certificate, not Betty's of course because she should never find out, so this kid thinks I am his father. His daddy. He doesn't even know about Betty, thank god. So, I tell him I am not his father, but here's this handsome kid who is the spitting image of me thinks I'm his father. And I am not. This kid looks more like me than you. Really tall for his age though. He's probably going to be an alchy like his dad. Betty said he was a real drunk. So I give him a couple hundred dollars and tell him to go home and forget about it. I'm not his father. He left, but this kid will be back to haunt me."

I know Betty will kill him if she ever finds out. And I think she should. Good thing she's away visiting her family in Pennsylvania for a few weeks.

"Betty will kill me if she ever finds out. Sweetie, where did you get that outfit?"

So uncomfortable in my own clothes, my own skin, my own soul, I have to look down at myself to see what I have on. Black jeans, black sweater, black boots, black jacket. I guess he didn't look at me this morning.

"Aren't you a little young for all that black? Where'd you think we were gonna go today, a funeral?"

He runs his well-manicured fingers through my hair.

"Jeez, Sha, your hair is shorter than mine. Let it grow a little. You're a little girl, for Chrissake."

I am saved from defending myself when the door opens and a heart-stoppingly beautiful woman comes in screaming at the top of her lungs. At my father. I cannot take my eyes off her. She must be a model or an actress. Tall. Red-haired. Expensive green suit and everything matches.

"Shiekie. You bum. Don't send me any more jerks like that hooziwatz."

"Geez, Gwen, not now, this is my kid. Sha, Gwen."

Gwen sits next to me and leans over and whispers in my ear.

"Shiekie gets me dates. He's a good friend. He never

fucks me himself."

I smell the peppermint lifesaver she has stuffed in the corner of her perfect mouth.

"Shiekie, your kid's adorable. Too bad this joker's your dad."

She spins around on her stool.

"Hey, Marco, come on in. Buy us a drink."

Marco carries a pretty expensive looking tennis racket under his left arm. He hands it to me.

"Here you go, a present for you, Shiekie's kid."

Gwen moves down to the other end of the bar with Marco.

Dad pours them drinks and when Gwen points at me he puts a Coke in front of me.

I sip my drink slowly from the cold glass bottle as my father whispers to Marco and Gwen.

Dad gives Marco some money. Gwen gives Dad some money.

He asks Marco if he broke into a nice car to get the tennis racket.

"Nah, assholes left the windows down."

"Sha, you like the thing?"

I nod, knowing I will never, never take tennis lessons, or play tennis, or even like it anymore.

"Then thank Marco and me for getting it for you."

"Thank you."

I sip my coke and wait for my dad's shift to end. I think about how much nicer this bar is than the ones my mother goes to and I am grateful my dad doesn't drink.

Ecuador

"Sha, your dad's a genius. Know what an Ecuador is? If the same jockey wins three races in one day. That's an Ecuador. Eck-kwa-door. You're almost 10, right? And half of 10 is five. Close your eyes. Hold out your right hand."

Five 100-dollar bills. He must have won big at the track yesterday.

"Don't give a penny of that to your mother."

We're going out and I'm all ready and waiting for him, so I walk around listening to his raspy voice echoing through the apartment as he sings over the sound of the shower.

"You must have been a beautiful baby, cause baby look at you now. I can see the judge's eyes as they handed you the prize."

There are no chairs in the three-room apartment. Not a single one. There's a table in the kitchen. No chairs. Two cardboard boxes, empty, and a bicycle with a flat tire are the only things in his living room.

"Hey, Sha, where are you?"

I go back to the bedroom and sit on the edge of one of the twin beds so I can see into the bathroom. He looks in the mirror.

"Who's the handsomest dad you've got?"

My mother is on her honeymoon with husband number three. My dad is definitely the best of the lot. They don't wear *Zizanie,* either. Too expensive. Dad splashes it on like it is free. When he's ready, the race begins.

"Hurry up, Sha, we don't want to run into any of those bastards."

Over the summers, I have learned who the bastards are. Aunt Sara and Uncle Al who live on the second floor, Aunt Millie and Uncle Marty who live across the lobby on the same floor, and my dad's dad on the sixth floor, front. There is a rivalry of some kind about the apartments, but I do not understand any of it.

It is hot out, but Dad lives just half a block from the ocean. The Boardwalk. The Beach. His apartment faces the Fourth Street Orthodox Synagogue. Right next to Gussie's Candy Store.

Dad takes my hand and we dash across the street. He does not want to see his dad, my zaydeh, who is in the shul praying with the other old men of the neighborhood. This is Shabbos. Saturday.

"Make a beeline for the candy store."

Gussie is my friend Freddie's mom and she likes me.

She hands Dad a scrap of paper as he lifts me onto a stool at the counter and heads for the phone booth.

"Gus, give the kid an egg cream."

A couple of summers ago, Gussie taught me how to make egg creams. Seltzer and milk and chocolate. And no eggs.

A cop stops in the doorway and waves to Gussie. She gets a funny look on her face. Intuitively, I turn to look at my dad. He sees the cop and stuffs the piece of paper in his mouth. He chews it elaborately and swallows it before he hangs up the phone and comes out to sit with me.

The cop shakes his head and moves on.

I slurp the last of the egg cream through a paper straw.

After lots of kisses and hugs from Gussie, we make our way up Fourth Street and turn left onto Brighton Beach Avenue.

Dad sees the look on my face.

"I swear on your mother's grave that this will take five minutes or less."

I scrunch my face into a scowl.

"My mother is not dead."

He swings me over his shoulder and carries me up the 50 steps to The Democratic Club.

"I need to give something to Mugsy."

Uncle Davey, Moe the Mope, The Brain, Mugsy, Cabby, Chick Glick, and a bunch of other guys play poker at tables stacked high with money. The Democratic Club, as my dad calls it, is a large open space that is so filthy he won't even let me use the bathroom there. Dad owes Mugsy money.

I try to hold my breath when we are in the club. Cigars, cigarettes, and sweat smells are stirred up by ceiling fans.

He carries me down the steps after he conducts his business and stops at the full-length mirror at the bottom.

"Look at us, Sha. We're beautiful."

We make a left on Fifth Street and walk the block to the Boardwalk. I love the Boardwalk. I love the ocean. We walk the rest of the way to Coney Island on the Boardwalk.

Dad stops every couple steps to say hello to somebody.

"Everybody knows the Shiek," he says.

I hear the old Jewish women say, "You two are cut from the same cloth" so many times that I finally figure out what it means.

We pass Hirsch's Knishes, Nathan's, the Parachute Jump, the Cyclone, and the kiddie rides.

"I've got a big surprise for you, sweetie."

We end up at the very tip of Coney Island. Steeplechase Park. A voice booms over a loud speaker through the huge mouth of a scary clown.

"Welcome to Steeplechase. I am the funny face of Steeplechase. Come on in and join the fun."

Dad knows I am afraid of roller coasters because a guy held me over the side of one once to scare my mother.

"This is different. You sit on a horse. It's a race. You'll love it and I get to watch from inside the tent."

I am afraid. But I like the carousel-like wooden horse. I am strapped on and my dad leaves.

I scream and hold on for dear life. I come in dead last.

The attendant unhooks me and points me toward the tent, but first I have to walk through the magic mirrors room and a room that tilts while the floor moves. I end up on a stage with a lot of other people. A wind machine in the floor blows girls' dresses up around their necks and two tiny clowns with mean faces laugh while one of them taps me with a stick that gives me a shock. Hundreds of people watch us all run and fall and try to get away from the clowns.

I don't cry, although I am scared.

I frantically scan the crowd to find my dad. He waves and smiles and I jump off the stage to sit with him.

He puts his arm around me.

"Watch. This is the best part. Watching the morons run around like that."

He takes out a nickel and a book of matches. He lights the match and makes the nickel really hot. He tosses the hot nickel onto the stage.

The clown with the stick that shocked me picks it up and burns his fingers. He looks out in our direction and throws the nickel back. He shakes his fist at us.

"You sick sonofabitch."

My dad doubles over with laughter. Everyone in the audience roars. My dad hugs me and whispers in my ear.

"You gotta have a sense of humor, never lose your sense of humor, Sha."

I love him. I will miss him. This time tomorrow I will be back in Akron with my mother.

I wonder if anyone will remember to pick me up at the airport.

Miami

On the plane ride home, I think back to 1949 when I was four when my mother and father and I lived in Miami Beach. Deco was newer then, but it was different and my dad loved the blue mirrors and stainless steel shapes. Sculptures of women were everywhere and the sun was always shining on the stark white buildings. Miami glowed.

My dad was a bookie and a numbers runner. We lived in his Uncle Jack's hotel, on the second floor, on Collins Avenue. Our suite was so small that my room was just a tiny alcove off the kitchen. Some mornings I'd wake up early and go out in my bare feet wearing only my nightgown. I'd go two blocks away to a mansion I'd found, slip through the slats in the gate, climb up on their fountain and watch the fish, the beautiful, glistening-in-the-sun goldfish. My dad put a stop to that when their estate manager followed me home one day and told on me.

My dad said, "Go to your alcove."

And he laughed and told the estate manager not to expect me ever again.

To the outside world our hotel looked like any other moderately-nice hotel in South Miami Beach, but Uncle Jack's place was the front for the biggest numbers racket in Florida.

On the first floor, the lobby level, in the back behind a beautiful winding staircase, there was a false wall that slid open to expose a huge room with tote boards, chalk boards with the odds for all local and national race tracks, football games, baseball, boxing, anything that could be bet on.

Sometimes my dad would take me in with him. I liked watching the wall slide away.

"Abracadabra," he'd say,

And I'd say, "Open Sesame."

When we were inside, the wall immediately slid shut. He would lift me up onto a high stool and go away to take care of business. I remember lots of noise, lots of smoke—mostly cigars—serious business. I wanted to write on the chalkboard, so my dad gave me a little one of my own. He taught me about the odds on horses and told me to never, never, never gamble.

And then I'd watch some more.

It was exciting and all the men liked my dad and asked him questions. When he went into another room with my great-uncle Jack, he would swoop me up in his arms and take me along.

"Shiek, you're doing a great job. I don't know where you get your energy."

Dad beamed. I beamed.

"But, Shiek, do you have to bring the kid in here all the

time? I thought you was putting her in school."

"Jack, she got kicked out of nursery school."

"Nice Hebrew school up the street?"

"That's the one, Jack. She accused a teacher of putting something in her orange juice. The teacher said she didn't. They went back and forth and my little angel here threw the whole glass of juice in the teacher's face."

"Shiek, come on, was there anything in it?"

"Yeah, cod liver oil."

"So, they kicked her out for that. Anything else?"

"I didn't like to take naps on those cots at naptime."

"She kept crawling under them and watching the other kids sleep. She was disruptive. Come on, doll baby, kiss Uncle Jack goodbye."

"That was a very bad thing to do, sweetheart."

My dad laughed.

I kissed Uncle Jack, but I didn't like him much.

Not long after that we left Miami. Just my mother and me. Dad stayed. I think it had something to do with Uncle Jack. Or maybe it was the hurricanes.

There was no sun in Akron. I missed Miami. And my dad. Akron was dark and smelled of burning rubber. There was no ocean. No hotel.

"Mommy, I miss school."

"Next year. Go outside and play."

"There's nothing out there but rocks."

"Then play with the rocks."

She dropped ice cubes in her glass and poured herself another drink.

Chapter 3

Grands and Greats

My great-grandmother's name is Annie Caroline Davenport Valentine Bramel. Carrie. So often my mother and I end up on her doorstep with no place to go and she always shakes her head, but she always takes us in. She scrubbed floors at the local children's home until she was way too old to do things like that.

By the time I was born, she was already in her late 70s and devoted to daily Bible reading and listening to religious music on an old record player.

She is a terrible cook and hands that skill down to her daughter and her daughter's daughters. She is proud to be paying for her own funeral, and paying for the plots on time for the rest of her family at Rose Hill Cemetery way out on West Market Street in the good part of town.

Grandma is my only connection with reality. She sits in her rocking chair near the furnace grate between the dining room and living room rocking back and forth and back and forth as she crochets her doilies or embroiders pillowcase and handkerchief edges.

On Sunday mornings, she dresses up and walks more than a mile to the Christian & Missionary Alliance Church on Lover's Lane. When my dad goes missing one summer in Miami, she takes me to Bible School every day because I can't go to Brooklyn like I usually do. I learn about Jesus and like the part best where he turns water to wine and feeds a lot of people with just a little bit of bread.

She worries about me sometimes.

I stay all night at Grandma and Grandpa's a lot. One night, past my bedtime, she tucks me in and leaves me alone in her featherbed. I love the featherbed, but I can't get to sleep. Grandma and Grandpa check on me several times and finally she comes back in, sits down next to me and gently asks what is keeping me up so late.

"The cartoons."

"There's no television in here, baby."

"I'm watching cartoons on the wall."

She leaves me alone in the room again and closes the door softly behind her. It doesn't shut all the way.

I watch a cartoon man kill a cartoon woman and drag her battered and bleeding body behind a gigantic rock. Then he runs away covered with blood.

My grandmother comes back with a cup of warm milk.

"Grandma, look, can't you see that man?"

I tell her what I am watching on the wall and she kisses me goodnight and leaves me alone in the room.

The next morning I wake up and hear my grandparents, Mom—I have to call her Mom not Grandma—and my mother talking in the dining room, just outside the bedroom door. It is a very old house and the walls are paper-thin.

"Calm down, all of you. She is not a witch. She's just a little girl."

"How did she see that murder while it was happening five blocks away?"

Grandpa shushes them.

"They caught the guy. It's over."

From that time on whenever I sleep at my grandparents' house, they give me paregoric in warm milk to help me sleep and to keep me from seeing things.

Grandma's Poor Little Sinner

"Bless this poor little sinner. Her mama's an alcoholic and her papa's a Jew, a Jew!"

I am standing at the altar of the Christian & Missionary Alliance Church on Lover's Lane in Akron, Ohio, because my grandmother is deeply religious at this point in her—already too long for her—life. As a devout Christian, my grandmother and everyone in her church think that Jews have horns and are descendants of Satan. She drags me to the Christians every chance she gets.

Today when Reverend Pilgrim asks for all those who want to be saved and to accept Jesus Christ as their personal savior to hold up their hands and be counted, my grandma grabs my arm and stretches it up in the air so far that I think it might come out of its socket.

"Come on down then, all you sinners. Come on down."

Grandma none-too-gently pushes me into the aisle and

before I know what's happening I am standing at the altar. It is Easter Sunday. Tall white lilies in pots covered with pastel-colored aluminum foil are all around the church and there are a whole lot of them at the altar.

I love my grandma, but this altar business is scary. I know it will hurt her if I don't do whatever it is they want me to do, so I bow my head and wait for what happens next.

Reverend Pilgrim stands above me at the podium. I feel even smaller than I am. I know this preacher because I go to school with his son, Billy. We are in the same class at Robinson school and this preacher's son sits just two rows away from me.

Grandma told me that Billy is an epileptic and for me to watch out for him.

I cannot keep my mind on the preacher's ramblings about my evil mother and Jewish father.

My mind wanders to last week in school when Mrs. Evans caught Billy Pilgrim talking to another boy in class. She made them stand up in front of all of us and then she put a big wide strip of white tape across each of their mouths.

I raised my hand.

"What is it, nosey Parker?"

"I need to talk to you alone, Mrs. Evans."

"Get up here, then."

I went to the front and stood on tiptoe to whisper in her ear.

"Billy is an epileptic. He won't be able to breathe right with that tape across his mouth."

The teacher glared at me.

"He can breathe. Go back to your seat."

I walked over to Billy and ripped the tape from his mouth and put it on mine.

Mrs. Evans was really mad.

"Take your seat, Billy, and let this little martyr here fill in for you."

Billy went back to his seat.

I heard the preacher asking me something.

"Do you accept Jesus Christ as your personal savior?"

I keep my head down.

Reverend Pilgrim comes down from the stage and puts his hand on the top of my head and then presses on my forehead.

"Kneel down, girl."

I kneel.

"Out Satan!" he screams.

And then, he says quietly, "Bless you, child. Bless you."

Everyone starts to sing, *"Jesus loves me this I know for the Bible tells me so."*

I whisper to Reverend Pilgrim.

"Can I go back to my seat now?"

"Yes, child."

I get up from my knees and race up the aisle to stand next to my grandmother. She has tears running down her face and she is still singing.

"Yes, Jesus loves me. Yes, Jesus loves me."

She puts a piece of candy into my mouth, a pink Canada mint. It fills my whole mouth and it tastes really good. This must be a special day for her. She usually gives me just the white ones, and keeps the pink ones for herself.

Great Grandpa Will

William Alexander Bramel gets short shrift here even though I spend so much time at his house with him and my grandma. He is a racist from Kentucky, part English and part Cherokee with roots in the Ku Klux Klan. When he was younger, he was a philanderer, an alcoholic, and he was good-looking and his wealthy family disowned him when he married my grandmother, an older woman. I can see that much of the insanity comes from his branch of the tree. My grandmother keeps him in line as much as she can. His brother died in an asylum for setting fire to his own house and watching it burn to the ground. His brother's wife and two sons died in that fire.

Grandpa is always kind to me. Firm, quiet and kind. He pretty much ignores me except on Friday nights when we watch the fights together on television. He pushes his lime green vinyl La-Z-Boy recliner back all the way and I squeeze in next to him so we can share the buttered popcorn my grandma makes for us.

"And now, the Friday Night Fights are on the air!" the announcer says.

Grandpa winks at me and I sneak over and turn the sound up a fraction. Grandma hates the fights, but she looks up from her sewing and sees that it's me turning up the sound and just shakes her head and goes back to her sewing.

I like boxing because it's fun to hear my grandpa shout at the TV. He gets especially animated when there's a white guy fighting a black guy. I smell booze because he sneaks Jack Daniels into his coffee, and he always has a cup of coffee at his side. My mother sneaks Jack Daniels into the house for him.

But Grandma knows and tells me, "No harm done. He isn't going anywhere at his age."

Early on those Friday evenings before the fights, when the weather is good, I sometimes sit on the red concrete porch steps—where I fell last year and knocked out my two front teeth—and watch grandpa trim the hedges. No fences for him; dense greenery blocks others out and keeps us in. I can't see over them because I'm small for my age.

One night a tall handsome black man walks through an opening between two of the hedges. He whips a small hunting knife with a red handle out of his pocket and slashes Grandpa's face. Then he runs away. He yells something at Grandpa that I cannot hear.

I scream and run to Grandpa. A little stream of blood trickles down his face from a gash on his cheek. He is very old and he has to lie down on the ground.

"Just for a minute," he says.

He reaches up and wipes his face with his hand and gets blood in his beautiful white hair. He won't let my grandma call an ambulance and they don't own a car. He just keeps hollering.

"Let that be a lesson to ya. See. See. What did I tell you? You can't trust a one of them. Give 'em an inch and they take a mile."

I already know he's wrong. My dad has lots of black friends and so do Grandma and I. Every Sunday night I go down to the church at the corner and sit outside listening to the Baptists sing gospel songs. They are too alive to be as mean as Grandpa thinks. And they never chase me away.

No, Grandpa did or said something to that man. Or maybe the hate in Grandpa oozed out onto Bittaker Street and hit that man as he walked by. Grandpa doesn't call the police, which makes me sure I'm right.

And whenever I see the man who cut my grandpa, he smiles and waves at me and I wave back. So does Grandma.

Grandpa spits on the ground.

Grandpa hates Jews, too. He tries to hate my dad, but fails. My dad is too good at winning people over and much too smart to let my grandpa bother him. Once, my dad sent Grandpa a picture of himself dancing with Bill Robinson, the famous black tap dancer that everyone called Bojangles. Grandpa cut Bojangles out of the picture. He wanted to throw the whole thing away, but he couldn't bring himself to do that.

Grandpa likes to tell me the story of the time he and my father planned to kidnap me when I was just a few weeks old and take me back to New York. My mother was out at work at a bar or drinking at a bar, he couldn't remember which, and my father flew into Cleveland Hopkins Airport from New York on United Airlines, showed up in front of the house on Bittaker Street in a cab at the appointed time, and my Grandpa had my clothes packed and me all bundled up in a pink blanket when he ran out to the cab and handed me over. Of course money exchanged hands.

My Mother's Mother is Known Only as Mom

She gave me a drinking glass once that her second husband had given her as a token of his love. It had a few words etched into it. "July 24, 1945. You forgave me last night. I love you. Bill." Mom told me the story.

Grandpa Bill Hartman beat her so badly on July 23rd, the very day that I was born, that she lost the vision in her left eye. She was marked forever and so ashamed that it looked bad that she wore tinted glasses for the rest of her life. Bill Hartman was a murderer out of prison on a legal technicality when they fell in love.

She told me her first husband, my real grandfather Everett Sidell, was a jack-of-all-trades. He played guitar and sang, he loved movies and theatre, but his real claim to fame was how much he could drink before he passed out. He proposed to my grandmother at the movies. They must have had a lot of fun before their marriage ended with his death at age 24. He worked odd jobs. I think his main occupation was as a baker, and he played guitar for a few bucks now and then. When he was too drunk to work, and he didn't want Mom to get mad at him, he would go into the bakery, throw flour all over himself, go home and pretend he had worked hard all day long. He loved my mother and even when he rode the rails during the Depression looking for work, he wrote to her and sent her gifts every chance he got. He must have been kind because he always sent Aunt Pat, my mother's little half sister a gift, too.

He spent his last day of this life in Cincinnati, Ohio.

Outside a sleazy bar, after he had had more than a few too many, he tried to stop a man from beating a woman to a bloody pulp. The man stabbed him to death.

My then six-year-old mother was put on a train all by herself to go to her father's funeral. Her relatives forced her to kiss him goodbye in his coffin and she remembers that moment even now.

Mom's three loves of her life:

1. Everett Sidell: alcoholic, my mother's real father

2. Lora "Red" Gaynor: alcoholic child molester and Aunt Pat's father

3. Bill Hartman: alcoholic murderer and wife beater and nobody's father

Those were Mom's three true loves, the ones she married, anyway. There were many, many boyfriends after Bill went back to jail. Mom was quite the romantic.

She is a flirt and a woman out of her element, light years ahead of her time, or way behind it, and completely out of her mind. She was born dirt poor and could not accept that fact.

She had no formal education and no ambition. She is beautiful, talented, funny, loves animals and people, and always has an aquarium, a cat, a dog and a bird. She spends all the money from her men on herself. She buys clothes and cheap costume jewelry, Esteé Lauder makeup and night creams and White Shoulders perfume. She has to have her hair done every week no matter what. She wrote a book once about the family and her father burned it. She can play any musical instrument by ear and has a lovely voice. None of these things help her in life.

Mom is self-absorbed, the ultimate narcissist, and she has a whole lot of fun. She loves my mother and Aunt Pat, but fears them. I think it's because of their mental problems and abuse of alcohol and drugs and the violence that follows them around. She drinks, but her daughters inherited their alcoholism and meanness from someone else in the family.

She lives with her parents, my grandmother and grandfather, in that little house on Bittaker Street.

She and her steely-eyed husband Bill Hartman—the one who gave her that etched glass—took me to Cedar Point, an amusement park on Lake Erie in Cleveland, once when I was about three. Lots of photos. She loved the camera. They took me on all the rides, bought me pink cotton candy and a green chameleon. The chameleon had a collar attached to a tiny gold chain, and I wore it pinned to my dress all day long. I loved the way it turned colors. My grandma accidentally cut that poor little chameleon in half when I was playing with it on the dining room table. She just meant to catch it.

Anyway, we had fun that day at the amusement park.

Not So Grand

When I am in Brooklyn one year on Yom Kippur, my father's father decides at the last minute to take me to the synagogue with him on this the holiest day of the Jewish year, The Day of Atonement.

My grandfather is vice-president of the synagogue on Fourth Street in Brighton Beach. The synagogue is directly across the street from our apartment building at 3093.

All the children in the neighborhood love my grandfather and they call him "The Zaydeh," which he always tells me is grandfather in Yiddish. He is my own personal zaydeh, but he doesn't like me. I've heard pretty disturbing stories about him from both my mother and my father, so I am leery of him, as well.

He is icy toward me and he says terrible things about my mother to anyone who will listen.

Over the years he has lumped my mother, Mom, Aunt Pat, and me into one basket of bad apples. He calls me the *shiksa*, the gentile. My mother told me once when she was really sad that zaydeh paid her to leave my father when she left for the last time. She said my dad never forgave him.

Why he decides to take me to shul with him, I do not know. He pounds on the door of my dad's apartment and tells me to hurry or we will be late.

My zaydeh is an orthodox Jewish tailor from Russia. He wears a yarmulke and prayer shawl and gray suit this morning. He is short with lots of gray hair and deep blue eyes. He doesn't look human to me. He is so perfect.

At our front door, he whips my purse away from me and throws it back into the apartment.

"No money is to be carried into the synagogue."

My father, wearing just a white towel with his initials on it in gold, comes to the door and says.

"Jesus, Pop, don't be so rough. She doesn't know."

Then he slams the door on us.

Now it's just zaydeh and me.

We cross the street and enter the noisy synagogue. He marches me over to the side where the women sit and plops me down into a navy blue velvety seat with shiny brass arms. He looks around, then down at me, and says quietly, "This was your bubbe's chair. We bought it in her name, may she rest in peace. You sit here. Stay with the *vimmin*." I mock him in my head, the *vimmin* the *vimmin*.

He leaves me there alone and joins the other men up front in the center. He is with the rabbi, the cantor, and some other old men. My father has told me about rabbis and cantors.

I am uncomfortable. I read the nameplate on my seat. "Golda." I shiver. It is my bubbe's seat. He bought it to honor her after she died. The women all around me speak Yiddish, or Russian, even Hebrew. Some smile over at me, but no one speaks to me in any language. I guess my zaydeh waited until I was old enough to read so he could show off the seat.

I look out into the crowd and track down my zaydeh. He has taken his place in the front row. All the men are talking out loud and all at the same time. Bees. They sound like a swarm of orthodox Jewish bees. Jew Jew Bees. Like the candy I like at the movies. I make myself laugh, but not out loud.

The synagogue is a beautiful place. It is nothing like my Lover's Lane Christian and Missionary Alliance in Akron. It is magnificent inside, and from the outside it looks so ordinary. This is a place for prayer, a place to talk to god, so I do. I close my eyes and pray to myself and wait.

The service begins, but the noise drones on.

Then the rabbi and the cantor go backstage and come out from behind a curtain carrying the Torah. It looks heavy. They place it in its spot. The rabbi speaks to us in English. I am so happy to hear my language. I relax as he talks about the year ahead and being good to others, even if they are not good to us in return. Then he prays in Hebrew. All the men pray along with him.

Afterward, I walk out with the women and wait outside for my zaydeh. One pretty and quite round woman bends over and squeezes my face.

"*Shana punim.* Benny's *ainicle.*"

"Shiekie's *shiksa,*" my zaydeh says to the woman as he appears at my side.

The woman smiles and tells him, "She looks just like the rest of your family. More so even than the other grandchildren. She is cut from the same cloth as you."

My zaydeh makes such a face at the woman.

The rabbi joins us.

"So this is your granddaughter is it, Ben?"

He nods to the rabbi.

The rabbi smiles.

"She looks just like Shiekie—and Golda—and a little like you, too."

"But remember, rabbi, her mother is from the drinkers, and a gentile."

The rabbi lifts my head and locks his blue eyes with my blue eyes.

"No shame," he says.

He smiles at me and I smile back.

We leave then and my zaydeh takes me to join the rest of the family at Aunt Sara's apartment. Aunt Sara is my father's older sister and she and my uncle live on the second floor with their kids, Francine and Kenny. Aunt Sara likes me. She gives me a big hug. Uncle Marty, Aunt Millie, Robbie and Merryl live on the ground floor.

"Sit here, *bubbala.*"

She walks me over to the chair next to my zaydeh's and directly across from my dad.

Halfway through the meal, I have to go to the bathroom. I push my chair out and my zaydeh makes a loud gurgling kind of noise. I push my chair a little more and he screams. His arm is caught between my chair and his. He can only scream. It's his bad arm, the one he hasn't been able to use since the stroke a couple of years ago.

I try to move the chair so it won't hurt him, but he screams again.

My aunt's face turns white as she yells, "*Oy, mein got,* don't move the chair anymore."

She hurries around the table and pulls me out of my chair from behind and lifts my zaydeh's arm from between the two chairs. He sits holding his arm and moaning.

I run down the long hallway to the bathroom. The hallway floor is wood and there are no rugs all the way to the bathroom. My shoes sound like horse hooves on pavement hitting the floor as I run, trying to make as little noise as possible. I sit on the toilet for a long time and think about trying to escape, but we are on the second floor, in the back, and there's no fire escape outside the bathroom window.

Eventually I have to leave the bathroom. I take off my shoes and walk slowly and silently to the dining room. They have moved my chair over by my dad's—opposite my zaydeh. Everyone is eating.

My zaydeh is still moaning, but not as loud.

My dad leans over and whispers in my ear, "Good move."

Chapter 4

Of Three I Sing

Halloween, Trick or Treat, Beggar's Night. It's still 1954 and I am still nine. I sit on the bedroom floor flipping through *Mad Magazine* and watching the trinity, as I think of them—my mother, Mom and Aunt Pat—put on their identical rabbit costumes, including huge white rabbit heads. They look like horror film triplets.

Aunt Pat looks over at me.

"Why is it taking you so long to grow up?"

I bite my tongue and wonder why they aren't dressing as vampires. The only difference I can see is that all they can see is their own reflections in a mirror.

I cannot stop watching them. I feel especially obnoxious tonight because I sense they are grooming me to become one of them so that they will have someone younger around to take care of them.

Under my breath I mumble. *You could dress as monkeys and go as hear no love, see no love, and speak no love.*

Mom hears a bit of what I say, but doesn't know what I am talking about. She puts her two-cents in anyway.

"Stop biting your fingernails."

I think they might really be witches. My mother, Mom and Aunt Pat. the Three Witches of Akron. That flaming red hair, their crazy eyes; the way they spend all their time together. They must share some deep dark secret. They plan their days and nights around each other. The three of them shop, eat, drink, party, lie and cover up for one another. They have no other friends, they vote on who stays and who goes husband-wise. All for one and one for all. The Trinity.

When they've finally gone, I go to my bedroom and lie down. I close my eyes and as I fall asleep I think again how lucky I am that my mother is my mother. How thrilled I am that I didn't get the totally crazy one or the completely silly one, just the really troubled and unhappy one who does the best she can.

My dream that night is vivid.

The Dream of Planet Orrs

I am in the middle of a meeting of the Elders on Planet Orrs, a planet I often visit in my dreams.

Zela and her husband Alez called the meeting because they are worried about the children of Orrs, especially their only child, Koko.

Alez speaks first when he says, "We, Zela and I, have come up with a way to entertain our children and teach them life lessons at the same time."

Zela cuts in.

"We will give each Orrsian child an Earth child to have as its very own. They can connect via those screens they like so much and they can watch their Earthling 'siblings' as they grow."

Alez asks if there are any questions, and six-fingered hands go up all over the room.

An elder turns his microphone implant up just slightly.

"What happens if the children get bored anyway, or lose their Earthling, or Goth forbid, break them?"

Zela quips, "*Que Terra Terra.*"

And the audience roars with laughter. Zela is pleased and Alez is proud of her. The greatest gift the Orrsians have is laughter.

Alez smiles at his wife.

"You know, Zela, this is not a completely unique idea we're having here. On my 10th birthday my own parents gave me three Earth women."

There is a click and everyone faces a large projected image on a screen. Three gorgeous red-haired Earth women appear.

"The oldest one is the mother; the other two are her daughters, half-sisters. They are the offspring of my father's original Earthlings. I made the daughters half-sisters for more variety."

A skeptical Orrsian woman asks, "How did you hook into them?"

"I had to take away the basic Earth instinct of being maternal. That's why we usually only do this with the women. It was simple. Maternal instinct gone; Orrs connection in."

An Orrsian male turns up his microphone and says, "How did you get them to focus only on themselves?"

"Their maternal instincts are weak. They anger easily. They distrust other women, men, and even their own children."

The Orrsians laugh out loud in disbelief.

A woman asks, "But what else is there?"

"They love themselves," Zela answers.

Alez cuts in as he advances the film.

"Notice I installed a shield thin enough for others to walk through, yet thick enough for my three women not to be able to feel anything when they are touched. I believe we should give the Earth children to our children who are capable of great love."

So each Orrsian child is given an Earth child. Some of the wealthier ones are given two or three, or even a whole family.

Koko, Alez and Zela's only daughter is given a girl related to the three red-haired women. And even though Koko loves her little girl, when she gets together with her friends, she tortures her for fun.

One day Koko asks Alez, "Daddy, can I kill one of your red-haired women?"

"No, my precious one, "Alez sighs. "You must not kill. Besides, the way I wired them, if one dies, they all die. Not necessarily physically, but psychically. Koko, don't feel sorry for that little Earth girl of yours, she has no feelings that matter. She can be whatever you want her to be."

Koko pouts.

Lassie Comes Home

I wake up to the familiar sound of fumbling keys in the front door. It's my mother. She still has on the body part of her rabbit suit, but the head is gone, her makeup smeared and she is only slightly less drunk than usual.

She throws herself down on the couch.

"Get me a drink and a wet washcloth for my head. And promise me you'll never put me in a nursing home."

I bring her the drink and put the washcloth on her forehead. I kneel down next to her on the floor and push her hair away from her face. The rabbit costume has the heavy scent of mothballs and her breath is all cigarettes and Seven Crown.

"Did you lose the rabbit head?"

She answers with a question.

"Is there anyone you'd rather have as a mother than me?"

"Mother, please, not this again. You know there is no one I'd rather have than you."

"Not even Susan Hayward? Debbie Reynolds? Ingrid Bergman?"

I keep shaking my head, and praying she will stop this game.

"You and your damn movies. I know there's someone."

I lean toward her to say no and she gently slaps my face.

"No, really, Mother, there is no one. You are the very best mother for me."

And then she not so gently slaps me one more time.

I stand up and move away from her and whisper, "Lassie."

She doesn't think she's heard me correctly.

"What the hell did you say?" she asks.

I step inside my bedroom and lean out to repeat, "Lassie. I wish Lassie was my mother."

Chapter 5

Oh Tannenbomb

I wait for them as long as I can. It is Christmas Eve, 1954. My little brother Bobby is tucked in his bed with visions of sugarplums—while I sit up and worry.

Staring at the boxes of decorations and strings of lights is making me crazy. My mother and stepfather, Bob, should have been home hours ago.

Where are they?

I turn on the radio and listen to carols being sung by the Mormon Tabernacle Choir, Johnny Mathis, and then Nat King Cole.

Our Christmas tree is propped up out on the porch. It's been there almost a week.

"The branches will spread, open up, fill out, you know, if we leave it outside for a day or two," so Bob said.

My mother and Bob are selling Christmas trees this year and expecting to make a bundle. So far, all I've seen is this one tree. It's pretty, though. Blue spruce, with long needles and it smells good, even out in the cold night air. Bob put it into its little red stand the day he brought it home.

I have stared at it long enough. I drag the tree into the house. It is not easy and little bumps pop up on my arms and face where the needles touch me. I guess I'm allergic to Christmas trees. Bob already made a place for it in the living room. It wasn't hard. There's not much furniture in there, just the big beige couch and chair we brought from the last place.

The tree and I are both happy to be inside where it's warm. I have never trimmed a tree before. Not all by myself. My mother said they'd be home early, after the trees were sold. She said if it got late, she'd give them away to people who couldn't afford a tree.

I twist the tree around and around until I find the best side, the fullest.

First I untangle all the strings of colored lights and then plug them together end to end. I stand on a chair and get the lights up as high as I can, but that's only about halfway up the tree. I plug them into the wall and am amazed that only a few are burned out. There are extras in the box and I find them. Four to a box. Little white boxes. I think it looks okay with the lights only halfway up the tree.

I prefer those small white or blue lights that don't blink on and off, but my mother likes the colors and the blinking. I unplug the lights.

"Deck the halls with boughs of holly, fa la la la la, la la la..."

I sing quietly so that Bobby won't hear me and wake up. I wish my mother would come home.

Now it's after one o'clock in the morning. I figure it's already Christmas Day, so I carefully hang the ornaments one by one. We don't have many left because the best ones always get broken when we move, and we move a lot.

I hang my favorite ornament in the front of the tree as high up as I can reach. It's the baby's first Christmas decoration. It's light blue with silver glitter on it. I think about maybe next year making one for myself that says Bobby's sister's last Christmas. Bobby's step-grandma gave this one to us the Christmas after Bobby was born— it looks delicate—the way Bobby looks when he sleeps.

"Oh, holy night the stars are brightly shining..."

We have one box of leftover tinsel, icicles. My mother always just throws the shiny bits of aluminum at the tree. I hang them one at a time at the very end of each branch, sometimes two, because I'm getting sleepy. I plug in the colored lights again and go to the kitchen to get some water to put in the little red stand so the tree won't catch fire and burn the house down. The linoleum floor is cold on my feet, so I hurry. I spill a little bit of the water on my Christmas nightgown, which is a too small for me, but I am wearing it anyway. I don't think it's that small, even though my mother does. It says "Peace on Earth," and has a lion and a lamb on it.

I check on my little half-brother. He is sound asleep in his blue jammies with the feet in them. He is so pretty with his blonde curls all messed up when he is asleep—and such a monster when he's awake.

Bob showed me where some gifts are hidden under their bed for Bobby, little boy gifts. So I pull them out and wrap them and put them under the tree. Only one is difficult for me to wrap. The red fire engine that he can sit in and drive by himself, around the yard. I know he will love it. I am going shopping after Christmas with my mother and besides we're going to Grandma's for dinner and there will be presents there, too.

Now it is three o'clock in the morning. I will wait up a little longer.

By four o'clock, I fall asleep on the floor near the tree with the colored lights blinking on and off, on and off.

"*You better watch out, you better not pout...*"

A little while later I hear the car pull into the driveway. I take a deep breath and wait by my tree.

I hear my mother's voice first.

"You moron! How could you leave all the goddamn trees there and go to the View Lunch? Now, we have even less money than we had before."

"I was looking for you."

"Well, you found me. Happy, now?"

They fumble with the keys as they open the door. I hold my breath.

"I can't believe anyone would be low enough to steal Christmas trees, for Christ's sake."

I am still sitting by the tree, waiting for them to see how beautiful it is.

They stumble into the room.

Bob sees the tree first.

"Jesus Christ, what is this?"

"I trimmed the tree."

And then my mother.

"Well, it looks like hell."

I watch my mother walk menacingly toward the Christmas tree. She is angry. Bob is angry. Both are drunk. My mother calls Bob a jerk and he shoves her backwards into the tree.

Because she is drunk, she falls. The tree falls. I hate the sound. I wonder why people cut down trees for Christmas.

The baby's blue and silver first Christmas ball drops to the floor and shatters into all those little slivers that will be so hard to clean up.

My mother giggles a little as Bob pulls her out of the mess. She has little bits of silver glitter on her face and a strand of tinsel in her hair. They leave the tree lying on its face in the middle of the room with the water spilling out of the stand onto the floor and all over Bobby's gifts. Looking at them, I'm pretty sure Bob's days are numbered after this mess.

"Go to bed, you little smart aleck."

I start to clean up the water.

"Leave that alone and go to bed, I said."

"Oh, Christmas Tree, oh, Christmas Tree, how mighty are your branches."

Chapter 6

Stepfather Two—Husband Three

Alvin lives across the street from the View Lunch in an honest-to-goodness boarding house. He has a bedroom with a bath. He eats his meals with the other boarders, men with names like Mr. Steve and Mr. Bill. Lonely old men with canes. Alvin is 22 and just out of the Army.

I have no idea how he ended up in Akron. He was born and reared up, as he says, in Birmingham, Alabama. All I know about Alabama is what I learned on a drive to Florida once with my mother, two cousins and my Aunt Pat. I could not understand a word anyone said.

Then one sunny Sunday afternoon, my mother surprises me by showing up sober at my grandmother's house where I am a semi-permanent houseguest. She looks closely at me.

"I guess you'll have to do."

My grandmother is in the kitchen fixing dinner.

"You're not dragging that child anywhere today, are you? It's Sunday."

"That's my business, Grandma. And I know it's Sunday."

I kiss Grandma good-bye and she stands at the screen door wiping her worn out hands on an old apron. She watches us walk up Bittaker Street away from her and toward danger, in her mind.

I am so happy that my mother isn't drunk and that she looks so pretty that I don't dare ask her any of the questions running through my head.

Finally she breaks the silence.

"You be nice to Alvin. He's a little bit shy. Honey, I really want him to like you."

I take a deep breath and hold my mother's hand as tightly as I can.

"How's Bobby?"

"Don't worry about your brother. He's just fine, spending the weekend with his hoity-toity grandpa and step-grandma out by the Portage Lakes."

We walk in silence until we reach the boarding house

across the street from my mother's favorite bar. Now I am as nervous as she is as we walk without speaking up the stairs to the second floor front.

"Be very quiet."

She knocks timidly on the thick wooden door. The door opens. This is Alvin. So this is the Alvin that I've been hearing about. My mother's new hostage. He kisses her on the cheek and shakes my hand.

I look into his blue-gray-green oceanic eyes and I feel like crying. There is a lifetime of sadness and pain and anger in them. I see me. I see that he will never hurt me and that my mother will bring him even more pain. She will eat him alive.

He is very handsome, of course. My mother despises ugly men and only spends time with them when she is very, very drunk. Alvin is slender, muscular, taller than my dad, about the same height as Bob. I stare at his perfectly ironed white shirt and then look around the room. It is tiny but tidy. His army uniform, pressed and ready to wear, hangs on the outside of the closet door.

There is a bride doll, almost as big as I am, propped up on his bed.

"Aren't you a little old for dolls?"

My mother squeezes my hand and I shut up.

"It's for you. I bought it for you."

He stumbles over his words. His teeth are nice.

I let go of my mother's hand and walk over to the bed. The doll is really wonderful.

"Alvin, you didn't have to buy her anything."

And she gives him a light kiss.

My grandma has been saving up to buy me a doll. I think she has one on lay-away, but this one is spectacular. I think she'll be happy for me and she can add the money to the plots she is buying out at the Rose Hill Cemetery, instead.

"Pick her up. She's yourn."

Yourn... I will have to learn a whole new language, but I love the doll and I like Alvin already.

They walk me back to Grandma's. He carries the doll and I giggle at that. It's a quiet walk because Alvin is not a talker; my mother is not a talker. My mother's rule for me is to speak only when spoken to, so I just keep looking at my first bride doll.

They leave the doll and me at Grandma's after Alvin is

introduced to her and Grandpa and Mom. We all wave goodbye as they walk up the street glowing in the late afternoon sun.

Poor Alvin, I think to myself. And I just know she is taking him to one of the private clubs that serves alcohol on Sundays.

The very next time I see Alvin is the day we move into the second floor of a duplex near Lover's Lane, just off Arlington Street about a mile from Grandma's. My Aunt Pat and her two kids, Michi and Michael, rent the first floor because she is between marriages. Now I go to Glover School for a while.

It is a quick move and luckily the place is furnished. It isn't bad either. I have my own room and it's not dark like a basement apartment. I think about maybe getting a dog. I am always thinking about getting a dog. Alvin says he likes dogs and my mother makes a face. The bride doll takes center stage in my new bedroom. I had to leave my horse, Dynamite, at Grandma's because Alvin said it wasn't fair to bring a horse, even an imaginary one, to a second floor duplex.

Our first night in the duplex, a bat flies through an open window into my bedroom. I scream like a banshee and Alvin comes running.

"You ain't afraid of a little old bat, are you, girl?" he asks.

He gets a spaghetti strainer out of a box in the kitchen and catches the bat.

"Don't hurt it."

He makes a home for it out of an old shoebox so I can take it to school in the morning.

We both freeze when my mother shouts.

"Alvin, get your ass back in this bed."

She tries to control her drinking for a while and is on good behavior, but it doesn't last. About a month later, she invites my Aunt Pat upstairs for a few drinks.

"I'm pregnant. Alvin's happy as a clam."

"Two kids are enough for anyone. If I get pregnant again, I'll kill it without a second thought."

Aunt Pat likes Alvin and doesn't like Alvin. She's attracted to him and looks down on him at the same time. The rivalry between my mother and my aunt and their men never stops.

That night I fall asleep early while the three of them are

only halfway drunk. Around midnight, I hear a thud. The sound of a body hitting the floor. I run to the kitchen. My mother is on the linoleum floor with deep red blood oozing from her tiny nose. She yells at me.

"Get out of here, you little snoop."

I try to get to my mother, but Alvin and Aunt Pat are standing between us.

In the morning my mother is all puffy and angry and Alvin is at work. I stay home from school to take care of her.

"That damned bat isn't still in this house, is it?"

"No. Did Alvin hit you?"

"None of your beeswax."

"Was it Aunt Pat?"

"Leave me alone."

It had to be Aunt Pat.

Later that day, Alvin drives us kids to dance class. He drives us everywhere. dance class, roller rink, library. He lets me ride up front and puts Michi and Michael in the back seat.

"Alvin? I think Mommy's an alcoholic. I think Aunt Pat is too," I say.

Alvin ignores me, and drops us off and goes on alone to the grocery store.

My mother is still in bed when we get home. She has an ice bag on her head. This is my clue she is drying out, which means she stays in bed and drinks only beer.

I start my homework, an essay on capital punishment, and in a little more than 10 minutes, I hear my mother's voice.

"Get in here. Please don't make me come out there and get you."

I rush to her bedroom. She stands by her unmade bed in the dark. Her eyes look funny.

"What did I do now?"

"What didn't you do?"

She hits me on the head with her wooden hairbrush. Hard. I fall. As I try to get up she puts her bare foot on my stomach to hold me down. I roll over and she hits the back of my head with the brush.

I am a mess when Alvin comes home from the store.

"Are you trying to kill the girl?"

"Yes, goddammit, I am. Did you get the beer?"

Alvin picks the brush up from the floor and puts it on her nightstand.

"They didn't have Schlitz, just Bud."

Alvin helps me up and looks me over carefully.

"She didn't hurt you, did she?"

I answer truthfully, "No, she didn't. Not really."

"What's this about?" he asks her.

"You know, you hypocrite. You agreed with her. That little snot told you I'm an alcoholic and Pat too."

"No, of course not, darlin'. You can stop drinking any time you want."

Alvin winks at me and shoos me out of the room. Then he closes the door.

I can hardly move. I make a promise to myself. I will never say anything important in front of my little cousins again.

Reason to Love

My brother Darryl is born April 30, 1955. It is the happiest day of my life. He is what I want, not a doll.

I wait at home with my out-of-control brother Bobby, now five, while Alvin picks up my mother and the baby at City Hospital.

All I can see is a cocoon of blue blanket as Alvin gently places him in the middle of their double bed. The baby's eyes match the sky blue of the threadbare chenille bedspread. His skin is soft pink. He doesn't make a sound. He just stares at the ceiling.

We all go into the kitchen. It's a celebration for Aunt Pat, her kids and Mom—and an opportunity for my mother to really tie one on. My mother makes up several bottles of formula for the baby and I watch carefully. I leave them all laughing and toasting each other in the kitchen and go back to the new baby.

"Don't fall, Darryl. I love you."

Aunt Pat hears me.

"That baby's not going anywhere. Come on back in the kitchen."

I ignore her and stay with Darryl. I feel something I have never felt in my life. I love him and I am frightened for him. He is so tiny. I touch his face, his head, his perfect hands. I kiss his cheek and whisper softly, "Don't be afraid."

He makes no sound. I fall asleep next to him on the bed where he was conceived.

Later on, the laughter from the kitchen alternates with arguing and fighting. The baby wakes and does not cry. I give him another bottle and change his diaper. The safety pins are scary, but I am careful not to stick him.

Just Across the Street

The continual arguing between Alvin and Aunt Pat escalates while I am in New York with my dad over the summer. When I come home, we are completely moved into a new place. It's a little white shack, referred to as a guesthouse, behind a bigger white house just across Bittaker Street, just across from Grandma, Grandpa and Mom.

My first night home, Darryl, Bobby and I are left at Grandma's while Alvin and my mother paint the town red. Of course the new house is walking distance from the View Lunch.

Sometime after midnight, Alvin picks us kids up and takes us home, across the street. He carries the baby and I hold Bobby's hand in the dark.

"Where's Mommy?"

"She'll be along right soon, now. Your Aunt Pat's droppin' her off."

Alvin is not an alcoholic.

We are all awakened around four in the morning. It is a free-for-all in the driveway. Aunt Pat hits and kicks Alvin. My mother hits Alvin. Alvin slaps my mother so hard it echoes in the night. I watch through the screen door for as long as I can stand it. My mother is getting the worst of it. She is not only the smallest of the three of them, she is by far the drunkest.

I take some change from a jar, and still in my pajamas, run two blocks to the nearest pay phone. No one sees me.

All the lights are out at my grandma's house, so I race back home to get there before the cops come.

My dad's advice about keeping change handy for payphones came to good use.

The flashing red lights and loud sirens wake the entire neighborhood as the cops pull into our driveway, two cars, one right behind the other. They shine more lights on the battling trio.

I stand inside the screen door to watch. One of the cops nods in my direction. I close the door and go back to bed.

Chapter 7

Hell of a Ride

I am determined to see the New Year in, but the steady blinking of the colored Christmas tree lights hypnotize me. I am half-asleep around 11 o'clock when I hear my mother laughing outside. After a lot of fumbling with keys, the door swings wide open. My mother and the man with her are wobbly drunk.

"Happy New Year! Happy 1956!"

The man picks me up and swings me around. It's Bob. The love of my mother's life and also my first stepfather. Alvin, my second stepfather, works the graveyard shift at the Ford Plant somewhere near Cleveland. That's where he is tonight.

"Start packing, kiddo. We're out of here. Move it."

Bob puts me down and goes to find the boys. My five-year old brother Bobby is his son.

"Pack goddammit, and pack the boys' stuff, too."

My mother throws her makeup and clothes into anything she can find. Shopping bags, old suitcases, boxes.

I get the baby's stuff first, then Bobby's. As much as I can stuff into two pillowcases. I grab a box from under the tree. A gift from my dad. A navy blue taffeta reversible skirt and a white see-through nylon blouse.

"For a party," he said.

Before midnight, we are packed and crammed into Bob's old brown and tan jalopy. Mother, Bob and the booze are up front. I have the baby on my lap and Bobby curls up next to me. The hi-fi, some records, a toaster, a large framed baby picture of me and a few bags of road food fill up the back seat.

It's cold in the car and my mother cuddles up to Bob and messes with the radio dial. Just a lot of static.

I fall asleep listening to my mother and Bob drone on about taking the northern route in case he comes after us. He has a temper.

By morning the good booze is gone and they are drinking the beer.

Bob says things like—"*Ichi Bon Toxsan* Number one."

He was in Japan once when he was in the Navy. Bob

drives and drives and the baby cries and cries.

"Shove something in his mouth," my mother tells me.

I give him his pacifier and his soft blue bunkie.

They keep up their— "Alvin will kill us if he finds us"—act straight through to Nevada, about 2,000 miles. Three days of cheap food, crummy gas station toilets and smelly diapers.

And the snow.

At a place called Donner Pass where Bob tells us a lot of people have died, he and my mother argue nonstop. The baby sleeps, Bobby gets carsick, and the temperature drops to 13 degrees.

And the snow.

A "Scenic View" sign catches Bob's eye, and he puts on the brakes.

"Everybody out of the car."

The arguing stops when my mother reaches her goal and blacks out, but that doesn't stop Bob. He picks up Bobby in one arm and the baby in the other.

"Let's look at the goddamn scenic view!"

It is a starry night, the snow sparkles and crackles under my slippers.

Bob staggers and nearly falls.

"Give me my baby brother, please."

I get back in the car with the baby before Bob can stop me. I watch as he teaches Bobby to write his name with his own pee in the clean white snow.

A few miles later, a cop pulls us over.

"You can't drive up here without chains on your tires."

He speaks only to Bob.

"Follow me, buddy. We're not far from a motel."

The policeman stays with us while we check into the Loveless Motel.

"You get you some chains in the morning. You know stuff's falling out of your trunk?"

"Yes, sir, officer. The latch is broken."

My mother, blissfully unaware of it all, is still passed out in the car.

Bob pays one night in advance. He carries my mother up to the room.

I crawl into one of the two large beds with the baby on one

side of me and Bobby on the other and the warmth lulls us to sleep.

When I wake up later that night, Bob and my mother are gone. I look out the window and am so relieved to see that the horrible car is still there. I remember then that we passed a bar—or "joint" as Bob calls them—about half a mile from the motel.

In the morning, everyone is in a better mood for some reason and we slip and slide and skid and laugh all the way to Reno.

At a gas station, my mother drags me to a payphone.

"Person to person to Shiekie. Make that collect, Operator, from his daughter Sharon."

After a moment, she yells into the phone, "Shiekie? No, it's me. Reno. Did Alvin call you? I left him. Reno. Yes, yes, she's fine, she's right here. I'm with Bob. Yes, *that* Bob."

She puts her hand over the mouthpiece.

"Ask for money," she whispers.

"No."

"Tell him you're cold and need a coat and that you stupidly left all your school clothes in Akron."

She shoves the phone up to my ear and holds it there.

"Hi, Daddy. Yes, Reno. Yes, a lot of snow. Mommy wants me to ask you for money."

She pushes the phone into the side of my head until it hurts. And then she snatches it away from me before I can say anything like I love you.

"Shiekie, you bum, your kid doesn't have a coat and there's snow up to her ass here. It's goddamn cold. We're broke and we're going to get killed if we don't buy chains for the tires, and the baby is sick. Western Union, downtown Reno. Thank you."

She slams the phone down.

We wait in Reno for the money to come. We have no more money for motels, so when we check out, we go to a coffee shop and sit and wait until it's time to go to Western Union. Bobby and I play war with an old deck of cards. Bob holds the baby and attempts to cheer us up.

"First your money, then your clothes. That's the way the story goes," he says.

We park outside Western Union and wait some more. They keep sending me in to see if the money has arrived from my dad. When the money finally comes, I sit in the car and watch while my mother signs for it. She looks so beautiful, even through the yellow and black letters on the dirty Western Union window.

"And you, my little princess, have lucked out again. Your dad is sending you some clothes to Sacramento."

"Sacramento? The capital of California? That Sacramento?"

She doesn't answer me.

The snow becomes torrential rain as we cross the California state line.

Four days into the New Year. I have never seen so much rain in my life; at least the windshield wipers work.

"Bob, do you still have those tattoos?" I ask.

"You remember them, do you? Well, sure, those are my two best girlfriends next to your mother and you."

I wonder if he remembers that I used to put clothes on them with finger-paints while he and my mother slept. Crayons didn't work.

He also has l-o-v-e tattooed on the fingers of his left hand and h-a-t-e on the right.

Bob drives faster and faster the closer we get to Sacramento.

We pull into a deserted Army barracks and stop in front of a shack with peeling paint and a stack of bricks instead of steps leading up to the door. Inside it's a whole lot worse. There's a dirt floor in the kitchen and the rain has come in. Then I realize it's all one big muddy room: kitchen, living room, dining room all in one. There must be a bedroom somewhere.

"Goddamn you, Bob, you lying sack of shit!"

"January is a bad month, darling. Rainy season. All's I said was that I have a house for us."

On Monday, I put on my new taffeta skirt with the navy blue, black-and-white plaid side out, my white nylon blouse over one of Bobby's undershirts, and a big yellow rain parka that must be Bob's. Bob drives me to school.

"You'll remember how to get home?"

I nod.

He kisses me goodbye.

I march into the school office.

"We just moved here from Akron. I am in the fifth grade. Please call Robinson School in Akron, Ohio, and ask for the principal there and she will tell you I get good grades."

I sit in the outer office and watch two secretaries type until noon. This new principal shares her lunch with me.

"My, you are small for the fifth grade."

She pats my head.

"I called your prior school and everyone in the office was glad to hear you're okay."

After lunch she introduces me to Mr. Person. I stare at the floor in the hallway while the she tells him my story.

"Choose any empty seat you want. Class, this is our new student and she came all the way from Ohio to join us today."

I choose a seat in the back. I love Mr. Person. My Savior.

Rain and More

Sacramento has a record year for rain in 1956. And it is cold. My mother and Bob drink and argue and drink some more. Bob does not get a job as he had promised. He says it's because of all the rain.

We have a charge account at the local market where we turn in bottles for the deposit. Every month, Bob gets some kind of check, but it isn't enough for all of us kids and maintenance booze, too.

"Honeybunch, go down to the store and get us a six-pack, okay? And put it on our account."

"No, I won't go. You go."

So, Bob always goes. And so our lives go, as well.

Tahoe

One Friday, I am in charge of the class at school while Mr. Person goes to the office. We are making paper Valentines for our parents. I am holding a pair of sharp scissors and showing the class how to cut out hearts. The boy in the first seat of the middle row hits my elbow as hard as he can and the scissors go through my lower lip, all the way into my gums.

The other kids do not realize that the scissors are stuck and they laugh at me as I run from the classroom to the girl's bathroom. For the first time I do not love the fancy spray waterfall sink in my California modern school. I jut my jaw into the cold spray and try to pull out the scissors. No luck. No blood. Mr. Person soon finds me and pulls the scissors out with one swift move. Lots of blood.

As I am about to pass out, he picks me up and carries me to the nurse's office. She puts some kind of butterfly clamp on the gash and tells Mr. Person to call my parents to come and get me.

"No, I'll take her home and tell them the whole messy story. It's all my fault."

"I'm fine. You don't have to come home with me. I'm fine. Really. I'm fine."

"I'll call your parents first."

"We don't have a phone."

We get into his car. I get sick three times on the way and throw up all over the outside of the passenger door. For the remainder of the ride, I watch the rain.

"This it?"

I nod.

We run from the car to the door. It is unlocked.

"Anybody home?" Mr. Person yells.

I cringe when Bobby comes to the door with the baby toddling behind him. They are both naked.

"Mommy went to Lake Tahoe."

Mr. Person steps inside the kitchen with me and writes his home phone number on a piece of paper.

"Call me if I can do anything."

The baby says what might be his first word, "Tahoe."

Where's Bob?

I stay home from school for a few days because my bottom lip swells up over the top one and half my face turns purple-blue. Also, my mother is not back from Tahoe and there's no one to stay with the boys.

On Thursday, a cab pulls up in front of the shack—as Mother calls it—and she's home. She pays the driver and walks right past us into the bedroom where she throws herself onto the bed.

"Where's Bob?"

There is no answer and Bobby and the baby crawl into bed with her.

Friday I get to go back to school. Nothing is said about my

absences and I sit down and start our new writing assignment. A play about poor children in Mexico.

That night Bob comes home. Bruises, a black eye, dirty clothes.

"She here?"

I nod.

He showers and fixes dinner for us and after a while he starts talking.

"Your mother didn't want to leave the bar. I did. I tried everything I could think of. A security guard asked if I was bothering her; if she knew me. She looked him straight in the eye and said she'd never seen me before in her life. I went berserk and grabbed her arm. She threw her drink in my face and the next thing I know the guard grabs me. Your mother let them take me to jail. I kept thinking she'd come for me."

Poor Bob. The second time around and he still doesn't know her.

Two weekends later they go back to Tahoe, while I'm at school.

To Market To Market

We have no food in the house and the note on the fridge says for me to charge some at the local market. I hate to go, but I have no choice this time.

The guy who owns the little market sees me coming. Bobby's beside me and I'm pulling the baby in a broken down red wagon with a squeaky wheel.

"Hi, honey, what can I do you for?"

He gives us each a Hershey's bar.

"We need food for the weekend."

"Now, honey, your daddy and mommy know their credit has been cut off."

I stand there staring at him. I will not cry. He shakes his head and loads the wagon with Kraft Dinner, canned soups, milk, butter, bread, and a dozen eggs. He adds the prices to our long list of charges.

The Train Ride Home

The next weekend we are on a train to Akron, Ohio. I wonder if Alvin will take us back. Bob is sick to death of us all, but he keeps Bobby with him to spite my mother and also to help her out. Besides he loves Bobby.

As Mother, the baby and I board a train heading east, Bobby cries. Then the baby cries. Then Bob cries.

Bobby is the one who is blessed.

The journey home to Ohio is long and exhausting. Mother drinks just enough to sustain her, but not enough to get drunk. The baby sleeps a lot. My mother will not get off the train when we stop at the stations along the way and says very little to me about anything.

In Salt Lake City, she finally allows me to get off the train to look around; a very kind porter says, "Come on, cute stuff, stretch your legs. You got plenty of time. We'll be here a good 45-minutes to an hour."

I see the Great Salt Lake. It is amazing. I wander around the clean and beautiful place. It is a breezy day and I think about not getting back on the train. I imagine what it would be like to live on my own in Salt Lake City. Then I think about baby Darryl and my mother on their own, and I run back to the train.

It is gone. I panic and run around like a chicken with its head cut off, begging complete strangers to tell me what happened to my train.

The porter spots me. I am crying.

"It's coming back, cute stuff, just had to go out a ways to change tracks."

I am so happy to see my sleeping mother and baby brother that I forget all about ever moving to Salt Lake City.

I watch them sleep for a long time, then stare out the window of the train. There is nothing out there and a lot of it.

Tales Between Our Legs

Alvin picks us up at the train station in downtown Akron, dumps my mother and me at Grandma's, and takes my baby brother with him when he leaves. Alvin loves Darryl but not my mother and I belong to my mother.

Two down. One to go.

Alvin calls me over to the car to say goodbye.

"Don't worry none about your little brother. I hired a baby sitter for Darryl and rented us a little old house over near that King School.

You can come see us anytime you like. Call and I'll come get ya."

I kiss my baby brother and Alvin goodbye.

After they drive away, I hear Grandpa tell Grandma, "That baby's a far sight better off. He should've taken the girl, too."

My mother is already asleep on the couch.

We are at Grandma's for a few weeks. I cry a lot because I miss Darryl so much.

I sleep with Grandma in the featherbed in the bedroom. Grandpa sleeps on a rollaway in the dining room. My mother sleeps on the couch and her mother sleeps in the puke-green La-Z-Boy recliner that grandpa watches television in.

That night in Grandma's soft featherbed, I dream again that the world ends.

Chapter 8

Aunt Pat

Sometimes Even a Vacation Isn't a Vacation

When Aunt Pat's third husband—Paul—buys her a brand new powder blue Cadillac Eldorado convertible, she drives over to Grandma's to show it off. She only recently married Paul, a short, smart, dark, handsome Armenian, who owns a popular bar over on East Market Street near Central High School and Akron University. Paul walks with a slight but interesting limp and, according to my mother, he cheats on Aunt Pat with college girls that hang out at his bar.

Talking down to my mother, as usual, Aunt Pat says, "Come on, sour-puss, let's take a ride to Daytona Beach. We can take the kids. Come on, it'll be good for you after all you've been through with Bob and Alvin and those boys. Come on, you haven't got a dime to your name, but I do. Please."

Aunt Pat wants to see her dad who lives in Florida. Her dad's given name is Lora, but everyone calls him Red. He was a barber, but now he has a ranch somewhere.

Aunt Pat is beautiful. Some, including my father, say even more beautiful than my mother. I disagree. She has that same auburn hair, but her eyes are a root beer color and her olive skin doesn't really go with the rest. I am uneasy when she is around. I know she is asking us to go to Florida because she needs someone to watch my two little cousins. It's okay because it is spring break. Michi's eight and Michael is seven and babysitting for them on the beach is a lot better than watching my mother drinking and passing out at Grandma's house.

They stick us kids in the back seat, get a roadmap from my grandpa, who always has a map and never goes anywhere, and we're off.

"*Shiksa* can wear Michi's clothes and you can wear some of mine. I packed for all of us."

Aunt Pat always calls me *Shiksa* to remind my mother that she was once married to a Jew. It means gentile, but she thinks it means Jew.

In the car, my mother opens the glove compartment and I see a pint of Canadian Club whiskey, which happens to be Aunt Pat's favorite drink—and a handgun.

"Is that thing loaded?" I ask.

"No. But we will be."

They laugh and laugh and laugh.

My cousins and I play "I Spy" and count cows and horses until we fall asleep.

We wake up a couple of hours later in Breezewood, Pennsylvania. It's the first stop after crossing the Ohio state line. The Breezewood Motel is sold-out.

The manager tells us, "There's one of them silver Air Stream motor homes out back. You're a family and I bet y'all can fit in there for one night."

I lie awake in the Air Stream thinking about the people who live in them always spotting UFOs and I pray that some aliens will come and take me back to whatever planet I came from. I remember hearing on the radio that they're always struck by lightning, those little silver things. I am glad it's not raining in Breezewood.

The next day and the day after that whiz by and we arrive alive in Daytona.

Our motel room is on the strand. We spend the first day on the beach building castles and digging holes to get to China. I bury Michael up to his neck in sand, but he doesn't like it and cries. The ocean makes me think about my dad. I don't think about him very often, but sometimes I just can't help it. I miss him.

In the early part of the afternoon, my mother and Aunt Pat go out to buy my mother a bathing suit because Pat's is too big for her. They come back with several fifths of their life support, fried chicken for all of us, and an ugly brown, old-lady bathing suit.

Sunburned and exhausted, Michi, Michael and I fall asleep early and our mothers go bar hopping and discover their latest home away from home.

Our week flies by. We are all suntanned and rested and no one wants to go back home.

Then a kind of weird thing happens. On my way to get a bucket of ice for them one night, I find a man's wallet full of money. I put down the ice bucket and head for the motel office to give it to the desk clerk. Just as I am about to open the motel office door, someone grabs my arm so hard it hurts. It's Aunt Pat.

"Where are you off to, smarty-pants? And where's the damn ice bucket?"

I try to tell her about the wallet, but she snatches it out of my hand, pulls me away from the office door and shoves me up against a palm tree while she counts the money.

She bends my right arm behind my back and marches me back to our room. On the way, she tosses the wallet in a trashcan.

"*Shiksa*! And I thought you were so damn smart. This means we can stay in Florida another week. Don't tell anyone. Not even your mother. Especially your mother. Do you hear me?"

She scares the life out of me. I will never tell anyone about that wallet.

The following day Aunt Pat has a surprise for us kids. Not only can we stay another week, she buys us tickets to a Beautiful Child Contest and we have seats right up front.

Halfway through the show, my mother and Aunt Pat leave, telling us, "We'll pick you up after. Be good."

We watch tap dancers, baton twirlers, singers and acrobats. Then they bring out the beautiful babies and I start to miss my Darryl who is cuter than all of them put together. I even miss Bobby a little bit.

The show finally ends and the winner is a little girl with blonde hair and blue eyes who is a pretty good ventriloquist.

"Little Miss Daytona Beach."

Applause and more applause. Then the lights go out onstage. The cleanup crew cleans up the mess the audience made.

Michi, Michael and I sit in our seats being good while we wait for our mothers.

It gets dark and no one is left but one security guard.

"What's with you three?" he asks.

"We're waiting for our mothers."

"Looks like they aren't here and I'm closing the place. What'll it be? Want me to call them?"

I take a deep breath.

"No, thank you, sir. Would you please show me where I can call a taxi?"

He shakes his head.

"I'll take you. Where do you live?"

"The Starlight Motel. We're on vacation."

Back at the motel, I tell Michi and Michael the story about Hansel and Gretel and watch them try to stay awake. They are both more beautiful than Little Miss Daytona.

By the time I hear my mother and Aunt Pat stagger in, my little cousins are sound asleep. I pretend that I'm asleep, too.

More of the Same

Aunt Pat gets bored with Daytona Beach and decides we should see what it's like in Jacksonville. We've never been to Jacksonville. Aunt Pat and my mother sing up in the front seat with Michael.

"Oh, we ain't got a barrel of money. Maybe we're ragged and funny. But we'll travel the road, sharing our load, side by side."

It takes forever to get to Jacksonville, so they have to drink in the car. They also stop at bars that have funny names like Hootch's and Barefoot's.

A few miles outside Jacksonville, Aunt Pat totals her new powder blue Cadillac in a six-car pile-up that's her fault. The police drive us to a hotel and tell my aunt not to leave town until they say so. Michael and my mother—who was holding him on her lap in the death seat—are slightly injured. Michi and I are fine and Aunt Pat feels no pain.

Jacksonville is dreary. My aunt and mother bicker all the time and Michael and Michi are antsy. And the hotel is miles from the beach. It's hot and humid and my aunt cannot believe what the police are doing to her.

"Why are they making such a big fuss when no one was really hurt?"

Aunt Pat calls her daddy who lives in Ocala now and he hooks her up with a shyster lawyer in Jacksonville who can get her out of the mess she's in. Her daddy, Grandpa Red, invites us all to visit his Black Angus Cattle Ranch to meet his new wife, Maude.

Aunt Pat settles her legal problems with bribes. They go out on the town to celebrate. They lock us kids in the hotel room. Double locks from the outside.

"We'll be back soon. Watch TV and be good."

When I am sure they are gone, I call room service and order

food for all of us. I tell them the door is double-locked and they'll need a key. I add a big tip to the bill for the room service guy and we eat like little oinkers. At my request and because of that really good tip, the room service guy leaves the door unlocked for us.

"Be sure and put the chain on though."

I smile and nod.

When my mother and Aunt Pat aren't back by dinnertime, I take Michi and Michael for a walk downtown. We find a Walgreen's Drugstore and sit at the counter and order double chocolate milkshakes. Our first really good time on the whole trip.

We get back to the hotel long before our mothers do. They are polluted. Now my mother wants to go to Ocala to see Grandpa Red. Aunt Pat says he's her father and now she doesn't want to go.

"Besides, he's not your dad anyway."

I hear my mother whisper, "Thank god for small favors."

The rental car, a black-and-white Oldsmobile, is not a convertible. There is no gun in the glove compartment and they are back to drinking beer and not talking.

Ocala

I fall asleep and sleep all the way to Ocala. The smell of fresh cow manure wakes me. Despite the smell I am really excited to see all the cows and horses. Michi and Michael are, too. It is a real ranch and it goes on forever.

Grandpa Red is not much to talk about but he seems happy to see us. Maude serves ice tea and wears a frilly apron and a frilly smile. She looks worn out to me.

At dinner, we sit at a long table and eat and talk and laugh. Aunt Pat and my mother drink with Grandpa Red. Grandma Maude sticks with her iced tea. The food is not half bad, and the mashed potatoes are delicious.

"The potatoes are delicious, Grandma Maude."

My mother tells me to be seen and not heard.

Grandpa Red and Aunt Pat nod approvingly.

Michael sleeps in one twin bed and Michi and I cuddle up in the other.

A rooster actually crows in the morning.

We wake up, wash, dress and go downstairs. We are all pretty excited at this point.

Grandma Maude is in the kitchen alone, drinking coffee.

"Why, you little hoodlums you, what are you doing up so early?"

She's friendly enough and fixes us cereal and milk before she sends us out to play.

"Grandpa Red is out by the barn."

We run out to see him and give him big morning hugs and kisses.

"Want to see some baby cows?" he asks.

Of course we do. He gets on the tractor seat, puts Michi on his lap right after he puts Michael and me on the biggest gray horse in the world. I have never been on a full-size horse before, just ponies at Kiddieland.

"Ever been on a horse before, sweeties? Well, don't you worry none, she's old as the hills and she just loves to follow this tractor. Maude always tells me get off my high horse and I just laugh and laugh at her."

This horse is a far cry from Dynamite, but she is real and I feel powerful.

"Hold on to me, Michael." I say.

My little cousin wraps his arms around me and puts his cheek against my back.

We follow Grandpa Red out to the middle of the cow pasture and he introduces us to three new calves. I fall in love with one and he says she can be mine. I name the calf Gorgeous George. Grandpa Red lifts Michael and me down from the horse.

Then he reaches up under my shirt and touches me. I kick him and he laughs and lifts my cousin Michi's shirt up and touches her too.

He laughs at us and chants, "Tough titty says the kitty but the milk's okay."

I start kicking him and try to pull her away. I finally get her away from him. Then I take each of my little cousins by the hand and run with them back to the house. We march right up to my mother and Aunt Pat.

"Grandpa Red is a pervert. He tried to mess with Michi and me."

My mother puts down her drink.

"Is that old man still up to that stuff?"

I stay away from Grandpa Red and keep Michael and Michi away too for the rest of our stay at the ranch.

Back Home Again

There is no singing on the way back to Akron. Just drinking, bickering and teaching us the lies we have to tell everyone about the accident near Jacksonville.

"*Shiksa,* you know we are counting on you. You're the oldest—don't forget. Do not say that the car accident was my fault. Do not talk about the drinking. Do not mention your Grandpa Red feeling you up. You kids and your imaginations."

We drive on and on. Aunt Pat picks at her, but my mother ignores her as much as she can. Just before Breezewood, in the heat of frustration, Aunt Pat slows the car down a bit and pushes my mother out onto the road. I see her roll over to the side and lie there motionless.

"She'll be all right."

I am hysterical by the time Aunt Pat makes a U-turn and we pick up my mother. She is not badly hurt.

"I'm all right." She tells us. "I'm all right."

"Mommy, do you need the hospital?"

"No, no, no, of course not, you little worry wart."

Six and Stones Will Break Your Bones

I think back to one night when I was six and Aunt Pat dragged me across a gravel parking lot. I couldn't keep up with her in her hurry to get to the bar where my mother was waiting. When my mother saw my new pink dress covered with blood, she could only say, "Your new dress!"

Aunt Pat hissed at her.

"It's only dirty on one side. She was running and fell. It'll wash out."

Aunt Pat was still squeezing my hand. I said nothing.

Weekend with Aunt Pat

One time I spent the weekend with Aunt Pat and her first or second husband, Roxy the grocer. Michi and Michael's dad.

While I watched Michi, aged two, Michael slept. I was

five. Michi accidentally pulled the grocery store front door shut on the index finger of my right hand. I couldn't get the door open.

"Go get Mommy or Daddy." I cried.

I saw blood and passed out. When I woke up there was a bloody blue towel wrapped around my whole right hand. I was sick to my stomach. My hand throbbed.

"You'll be fine."

Aunt Pat put a clean towel around my hand and I saw my mangled finger.

"It's okay," she said

We left for Uncle Roxy's bowling tournament and I sat in a red leather booth and watched. Sometimes I passed out for a little while. Then I would come to and watch them some more.

The next day, my mother came to get me. She was horrified and rushed me to Children's Hospital. Too late to reconstruct, but they fixed the break as best they could.

Chapter 9

A Short Chapter On Getting By

Ardith, a barmaid my mother meets—who has two daughters—rents a house with us. Ardith is okay, but she drinks as much as my mother. They don't argue at least. They commiserate. Soon, mother is working as a barmaid, too.

Ardith's daughters, Denise and Debbie, show me how to masturbate and teach me how to kiss on the lips. All of us girls sleep in one bed and hold each other close during the nights we are left alone.

Ardith doesn't do as well as my mother in tips so she is always, as my mother likes to say, "up to her eyeballs in hock." She even hocks jewelry to my mother. Nothing really expensive, but you can see she cares about the rings and things, that they mean something to her.

Within a month, Ardith meets a guy and off she goes with him and her daughters, without any notice. She leaves my gullible mother with an apartment she cannot afford.

We have to move. I learn we have moved from the house that we can't afford when I come home for lunch one day and everything is gone. On the walk back to school, I knock on my friend Anthony's door and his mother lets me in.

"May I have lunch here, Mrs. Anthony?"

She remembers me from a school play that Anthony and I were in. He played Abe Lincoln and I played his wife Mary Todd.

"Come in, Sharon."

She asks me no questions and puts a bowl of hot Campbell's tomato soup in front of me. She gives each of us a chocolate chip cookie as we leave.

"You come back after school if you need to, honey. Promise?"

"I promise."

Anthony tells me on the way back to school that he can't walk with me all the way because I'm white and his friends make fun of him.

My mother and her mother pick me up after school. I have never been so happy to see them in my whole life.

Chapter 10

Sideshow

The very next summer, my dad returns from wherever he's been hiding out and asks me to spend the summer with him. I am worried about my mother and tell him so, but he wants to see me. And my mother definitely wants me to go. So, I go.

Mugsy and Dad meet me at Idyllwild Airport. They literally draw a crowd. Everyone thinks they are celebrities. My dad is so handsome and they are so loud. Mugsy and Dad have been friends forever.

The apartment in Brighton Beach is exactly the same—only cleaner. My stepmother, Betty, is 20 now and even more gorgeous than when I first saw her. Long black hair, eyes like coal. She is happy to see me again. I can feel it down to my toes. And now there are two beautiful babies, a boy and a girl, my brother and sister—Sandy and Vicki. They were born a little more than a year apart.

Betty and I spend just about every day of the summer out in the world with Sandy and Vicki. They look enough alike to be twins—especially when they're in their double stroller. I look like a snowflake among the three of them with their suntans, black hair and dark, dark eyes.

I love the babies. They are so good all the time. People stop us on the street to *ooh* and *aah* over them. At the beach one day, a photographer from *The Daily News* thinks Vicki is so cute that her picture shows up on the front page that very next Sunday as an example of how cute you can be during a major heat wave. We are regulars on Bay Four, the beach at the end of Brighton Fourth Street.

When we tire of the Atlantic Ocean or the sky turns a gloomy gray, we walk to Coney Island via the boardwalk and have hotdogs and French fries and orange soda for lunch at Nathan's. Then we all ride the carousel, even Betty.

This feels like a real life to me.

One day Betty asks, "Honey, if I leave you on your own in Coney Island, you'll be all right, won't you? You know your way around enough now, right?"

"Sure, Betty. I love Coney Island."

Not too many days after that, we walk to Coney Island, the four of us, and Betty stops in front of the Cyclone, the biggest and scariest roller coaster on earth. She hands me a wad of money.

I count it.

"Twenty dollars?"

Betty gives me a quick hug and stares at me for a minute.

"Let's see, it's 11 now. Meet us back here in front of the Cyclone at five. Okay, honey? Be good now."

At first I just watch Betty and the babies as they walk away. Her red tank top and white short-shorts look pretty in the sun. Her long black hair swings back and forth and back and forth with her movement as she pushes the stroller up Stillwell Avenue and then turns right. I play Skee-ball in an arcade where I earn enough points to get a tiny Teddy bear for Sandy and a fuzzy pink bunny for Vicki.

I remember that the sideshow is in the alley across from Nathan's—next to the frozen custard place. I have always wanted to go in there. The man outside who is dressed as a clown motions toward me.

"You won't believe your eyes," he says. "Come on in and see the smallest woman in the world. See Jo-Jo the dog-faced boy. Something for everyone. Come on in."

I pay my quarter and go inside.

The place is pretty empty, so I sit down in the second row alone and wait.

I am excited about this dog-faced boy, but first it's Lena Medina, a very tiny woman who gave birth to a normal-sized baby when she was just eight years old. She is even smaller than I am. She wears a silky blue dress and really tiny high heels and heavy makeup. She walks back and forth across the stage.

Jo-Jo the dog-faced boy is next. He doesn't really look like a dog. He looks like a very sad man with floppy ears and a snout and buckteeth. He wears regular clothes, too. He looks nice though and he waves to me. I wave back and he smiles.

I stay all day at the sideshow. At the end of each performance, I leave and then pay another quarter to go back in for the next show.

After the fourth show of the day, the smallest woman in the world comes out and sits down right next to me.

"Are you all right, little girl?" she asks.

"Yes, I'm fine."

"Then why aren't you outside playing like other kids? It's a beautiful day."

"I like it here."

"What's your name?"

"Sharon," I reply

"Sharon, I'm Lena."

"I know."

Lena shakes her head and goes back behind the curtain. At four o'clock, the sideshow shuts down for dinner hour. All the lights go out and I have to leave with everyone else. I still have an hour before I can meet Betty, so I am standing outside when Jo-Jo and Lena come out together.

"You're still here? Come on then."

Lena takes my hand. I feel very tall.

"Jo-Jo, Sharon. Sharon, Jo-Jo."

We go to a little room at the back of Nathan's and have what they call an early-bird dinner. They treat me like they've known me forever and let me listen to their stories. I am very quiet.

About 15 minutes later, Sammy from the carousel joins us and he remembers me from other days.

"Hey, kid, good to see you. How's that good-looking mother of yours?"

He gives me four gold rings that are good for free rides at his carousel.

"Bring your mom and come to the carousel again sometime."

People stare at us and some of them even laugh at Jo-Jo and Lena, but it doesn't seem to bother them at all.

"We're used to it."

They sign autographs and pose for pictures with their fans. One man asks Jo-Jo to bark, but he won't do that.

"Anything but that," he says.

By then it is almost five, and I have to meet Betty and the babies. I leave the three of them at the table still laughing and talking as I go.

"I'll come back the next time I come to Coney Island," I tell them.

I meet Betty and the babies at the spot where we had

parted on Stillwell Avenue in front of the Cyclone. She is exactly on time. I am very happy about that. I show her the gold rings and try to give Vicki and Sandy the stuffed animals I got for them, but they are both sound asleep.

"Don't tell Daddy I sent you off by yourself, okay, sweetheart?" she whispers.

"I won't."

"Did you have a good time?"

"Yes."

"Did you have enough money?"

"Sure."

We go back to Coney Island the next day and the day after that. I keep my promise and spend my time and my money at the sideshow.

One day I see Betty meet a man about a block away from the Cyclone. He is a policeman on horseback. She walks beside the horse, pushing the stroller. I watch until they disappear around a corner.

Lena and Jo-Jo seem to enjoy spending their dinner hour with me. Jo-Jo looks young, but he turns out to be 40. Lena is 50, but she doesn't look that old.

"I bet you thought I was just a puppy," Jo-Jo says, and we all laugh.

I use my gold rings at the carousel and ride free four times. Betty and the babies never go back with me, but Sammy doesn't say anything about that.

All summer long, Betty, the babies and I manage to be home when Dad gets there. We all go out to eat at a luncheonette on the Avenue.

Betty makes up stories about all the fun we had that day.

I never tell my Dad the secret of how I really spent my days at Coney Island.

Chapter 11

The Disabled American Veteran's Club On East Market Street

My mother gets a job at the Disabled American Veteran's Club—better known as the DAV—tending bar.

"It's a good place," she says. "They are open Sundays and can serve alcohol legally because it's a private club."

Ed, the owner or manager, is in love with her and so she can do no wrong. That's a good thing about the DAV, too, because we have no other money coming in from anywhere else now.

My dad is avoiding us again due to a huge gambling debt and probably depression, but my grandfather, the Zaydeh, won't give me my dad's new unlisted phone number or even ask him to call me. My mother curses at Zaydeh.

"You don't know the number either, you old pervert."

Then she hangs up on him. I like that. And she laughs. She has a wonderful laugh and a beautiful smile now, but for some reason she always puts her hand over her mouth when she laughs or giggles.

According to what my mother calls Savings Time, we live on Jewett Street for a long time. The mornings are uncomfortable sometimes because every once in a while there is a strange man in bed with her and even though I tiptoe around and they don't wake up, I see them. And smell them. She has run the gamut of Bobs. Bob Vallee, Bob Borden, Bob Richards. All nice Bobs, I guess. Bob Vallee bought me *Tabu* for my birthday. I poured it in the toilet and saved the bottle. The bottle is nice. Bobby Borden is rich and talks to me like I'm a buddy of his. I like him. He is the only blonde and he really likes my mother. She dumps him. He doesn't drink the way she likes to drink.

Bobby Richards takes me out on Saturdays while my mother works a second job as a waitress at the All Nations Club out on Massillon Road near the lakes. He's about 60, quiet and kind, and he seems to like feeding the ducks as much as I do. She dumps him right after she abandons his creamy white

Chrysler Imperial in traffic one day when it gets too hot out for her, and the line of cars becomes unbearable.

One winter morning, I wake up to find Uncle Roxy's brother in bed with my mother. He is married and on top of that his son is in the same grade as me. The smell of her room that morning—the booze the sex the sweat the garlic—makes me sick to my stomach.

"Hey, kiddo. How's life treating you?"

I don't even answer him.

None of the others were married or if they were she never mentioned it to me. For some reason, this feels like a step down.

On the way to school, I remember I want to ask what Grandpa meant when he said that all the furniture in the Jewett Street apartment fell off a truck. The fabric is nylon-looped and it's beige and square—furniture so big I cannot imagine how it could fall off a truck.

I'm in the seventh grade. I make my first real friends and love my social studies teacher so much that I volunteer to assist him with the basketball team. He's the coach, too. Jim Weiss is fresh out of college, a football player who knows zero about being a teacher. He's smart though. He teaches one year and then goes into retail. I love this year. Mr. Weiss hangs out at my uncle's bar. He's also my cousin Bob's friend, so I learn all I can about my hero. I get all A's again, but this year is different. I have a great English teacher, too—Mrs. Hershberger. My life changes because she believes in me. I do all my writing assignments based on the nightmares I have on a regular and often recurring basis.

"Very creative. A+," she writes. I'm in heaven.

I walk all of my friends home after school, and then walk myself home. I am afraid someone might want to come in and use our bathroom or something. It is always anything-can-happen day at our place or guess-who's-spending-the-night. I'd die if anyone ever wanted to walk me home or even come into our apartment for a glass of water.

Chapter 12

More Living to Do

My mother's drinking gets worse and finally becomes her entire life. She is barely able to work even a few hours a week at the DAV. She is drinking herself to death. There is no pretense anymore, drinking anything and everything.

"It all goes to the same place," she says.

If she doesn't want to be sick all the time, she has no choice but to keep on drinking.

Dad sends child support every once in a while. It isn't much, but it helps pay the rent on our basement apartment on Jewett Street.

One weekend we are so broke, Aunt Pat sends a cab for us and we go over to her house for dinner. A fight breaks out when Aunt Pat accuses my poor mother of flirting with her husband. Nothing could be further from the truth. She's just used to flirting with bartenders and drunks at the bar. And he is, after all, a bartender. My mother says a few choice words to Aunt Pat, then calls another cab.

Before I realize I'm not going with my mother, she kisses me goodbye, slams the front door behind her and heads for the waiting cab. Aunt Pat opens the door and throws money after her. It's too late for it, but she yells one of the family slogans anyway.

"Don't let the door hit you in the ass on your way out."

The cab with my mother inside disappears. No one can track her down and I am stuck at Aunt Pat's house. Again. Every night after that, Aunt Pat wakes me up when she has had more than enough to drink, and yet another fight with her husband about my mother.

"Your mother is a whore," she tells me. "You'll turn out just the same. You're just lucky, *Shiksa*, that your father's a Jew. That's what makes you think you are so goddamn smart. But it won't last, honey. It won't last forever. You'll turn out just like your mother."

Grandma files a Missing Person's report.

Aunt Pat makes me stay at her house instead of going to Grandma's, so I miss a lot of school. I hate to miss school, and when she finally gets sick of my whining, she lets me register at the school near her house—because she isn't about to drive me all the way to Fraunfelter at the other end of town. So, I attend Jennings Junior High School's eighth grade for a while. I make one friend there. She has red hair just like my mother's.

I am at school about three weeks later when Aunt Pat accepts the charges on a collect call from my mother. She is in Baltimore. She has no money. She doesn't know how she got there.

"*Shiksa,* your mother is all right," she says. "She's got lives like a goddamn cat. We're sending her money to get on a Greyhound bus and come home. She is safe."

"She isn't sick, is she?" I ask.

"No sicker than usual, *Shiksa.*"

Aunt Pat On My Mind

Winter. 1958. Akron, Ohio. I am spending another weekend with Aunt Pat, her husband Paul, Michael, and Michi. I will be in the ninth grade next year, high school. I look forward to it—that and being older.

Aunt Pat keeps her gun with her and loaded all the time now.

I watch from the upstairs window as the clean white snow piles up in the yard. Michi, Michael and I are dying to go out and make angels and build a snowman.

"Go on, then, get out there and act like idiots," she says.

The air is pure and clean and there is no sound but our laughter as we lie on our backs in our heavy winter coats and boots and move our arms up and down and up and down to make the wings of angels in the soft snow. We build a perfect snowman and give him a stick for a nose. We stay outside until the cold wet air freezes and makes the hair in our noses tingle when we breathe.

"Get in here, the three of you, you're soaking wet."

We are exhausted and fall asleep early, right after dinner, chicken and rice pilaf.

Later on that night Michael, Michi and I wake up and hear Aunt Pat and Paul screeching at each other. We listen as Paul rips the hi-fi cord from the wall and then smashes what sounds like the whole unit to the floor.

By the time I get downstairs, Paul is holding the hi-fi, wires and all, and is ready to throw the whole mess out into the front yard.

Aunt Pat points the gun at Paul.

"I should kill you, you ugly crippled son-of-a-bitch," she screams.

Michi and Michael run downstairs now and stand behind me. I am afraid for all of them.

Aunt Pat squeezes the trigger and the sound echoes all around us. She misses Paul and shatters the glass in the front door. The bullet buries itself in our snowman.

"Thumpity-thump-thump, look at Frosty go. Now, you two go back to bed," I whisper to Michi and Michael.

I hear their little feet as they run upstairs and can also hear Michael singing,

"Frosty the Snowman..."

"Give me the gun, Pat," I try to sound really mature when I say this.

"Go back to bed before I shoot you, too."

Paul, outside now, yells as he slips and slides to his Cadillac, wires and bits of the hi-fi falling behind him in the snow.

"This is the last time you'll see me," he shouts from his car.

"Good," Aunt Pat replies.

And she slams the door.

She turns and gives me a hug. She is so drunk she is barely able to stand.

"Give me the gun, Pat."

This time she puts it into my hand. I hate the feel—the warm metal. It's not as heavy as I thought it would be. I don't know how to unload it or where to put it. Anywhere will be better than in Aunt Pat's hand. After she passes out, I stand on a kitchen chair and get one of her heavy red casserole pots out of the cupboard. I put the gun into it for safety. Everyone's safety.

Chapter 13

Down by the Seaside

Something inside of me dies the day I turn 15. I have so many faces I can count on. I have one face for school. One for home. One for myself when I am alone. Today I feel like one of those evil-looking clown puppets that someone has thrown into a dark corner, out of sight. Out of mind.

I am in Brooklyn spending the summer with my dad. I stare vacantly into space until he says something to animate me. I am nothing by myself. No dreams. No goals. The voices in my head are with me all the time—and they will not shut up. They want me to cry.

"What makes you think you can do that?" the voice asks. "Don't get your hopes up. Expect the worst and you'll never be disappointed. You can't count on anyone. Don't make me laugh. Just give up."

My dad and his second wife Betty separated after she got out of the asylum for the second time. "No more," she said, and took the kids with her to live in a private community called Seagate at the very tip of Coney Island.

It's Friday night. My father is away for the weekend. He had to go upstate New York to Monticello Race Track or Saratoga, one of them, for a very special race. A race he cannot miss.

I didn't want him to go. I didn't want to be alone. I wanted to go with him, or stay with Betty, but what I said was, "I don't mind, Dad. I'll be fine. I'm alone a lot. All the time. I'll be okay, really."

I sit quite still for a long time after he leaves. Then I walk into the bathroom, look at today's face in the medicine cabinet mirror, stick my tongue out at myself and stare. My eyes are blank.

After that I open my dad's medicine cabinet. It isn't like home, that's for sure. But it will have to do. I take out a bottle of Anacin and a bottle of St. Joseph's Aspirin for children and a prescription bottle of something that Betty left behind. Probably something for her migraines.

I take my stash and go back to the kitchen.

Under the sink, there is a wooden crate holding empties and a couple of bottles of orange soda. I think it is so great that soda is delivered to dad's apartment every other Wednesday. I choose a room-temperature bottle of orange soda. I unscrew the top from the St. Joseph's bottle, dig out the cotton and line up the little orange pills on the tabletop. I sit on the floor; the faded linoleum is perfect.

I reach up and methodically take one pill at a time.

One orange aspirin. One sip of orange soda.

I take all the pills and sit on the floor feeling nothing.

I lie down. I stare at the ceiling and watch a large cockroach on its ancient journey. They're amazing. The exterminator comes every two weeks and it means nothing to them. Cockroaches are forever. You can count on them.

"Goodbye, Mother. Goodbye, Dad," I whisper to the cockroach.

I look down at myself and see that I'm wearing navy blue shorts and a blue shirt and I'm barefoot. Appropriate, I think, for the next world, whatever it might be. I think about how ghosts in the movies and on television have to wear the same clothes forever and I hope I'm dressed all right.

Now I am ready for the Anacin, the big white ones. One at a time. Sip, swallow, sip, swallow. Until they are all gone. The tabletop is empty.

And then I wait.

And wait some more.

Nothing happens so I take all the pills left in the prescription bottle and stuff the handful of them into my mouth. My pie-hole as one of my mother's boyfriend's calls it. I follow that with a big swig of orange soda and swoosh it all around.

And then I vomit, and vomit, and vomit again.

Everything is orange. Orange. Orange all over the kitchen. I am covered in orange smelly vomit and I cannot control it. The gagging and the horrible smell keep me conscious.

I cannot even kill myself.

I lie in my own mess, crying, gagging, and vomiting some more. Then I crawl on my hands and knees to the bathroom, to the toilet, to throw up again.

It seems like hours later when the vomiting stops. I am very much alive and very tired.

Before I go to bed, I clean the kitchen and bathroom; the thought being that I might still die, and I wouldn't want my dad to see this mess.

It could still happen. It could be a delayed reaction.

I toss the evidence of my failure in the incinerator down the dark hall, on the left, just outside the apartment. There is not a single solitary person in that hallway. No sounds in the building. I think for a minute that I have gone deaf.

Back in the apartment, I get into bed naked as I've destroyed my suicide outfit with vomit and I don't want to ruin anything else. I lie in a fetal position and half-laugh myself to sleep.

The last thing I hear from my voices is, *"Mr. Sandman, bring me a dream. Make him the cutest that I've ever seen.* You couldn't even kill yourself. Loser."

I sleep from Friday night until Sunday morning. The phone never rings. No one even knocks on the door. On Sunday morning, my vomit turns from yellow to pale green—then all that comes up is a clear liquid. My throat hurts, my head hurts. All those aspirins, and I end up with a headache and a lot of pain in my stomach.

I am empty and not dead. It is harder to die than I thought it would be. I am embarrassed by my pitiful attempt and swear never to tell anybody about it.

After I shower and dress, I spray Lysol disinfectant all around the apartment before my father comes back on Sunday night. He walks in and smiles his Shiekie smile, the fake one. I manage a smile back and ask him.

"Did you win?"

He shakes his head, "Nah. Let's go get something to eat. I'm feeling kinda empty."

Chapter 14

Happy Mother's Day

I am making good friends now.

My mother is further away, mentally.

She sees Leonard Zito, her new boyfriend, off and on. He is a really nice man although quite different from her previous boyfriends and husbands. She spends more and more time, however, with her real love, Seagram's Seven Crown.

Earlier today, the day before Mother's Day, my best friend Diane DeMali and I went shopping for gifts. Diane's mom is divorced and works as a bookkeeper at Yanko's, a restaurant downtown, so she drops us off at Polsky's Department Store on her way to work. She is overly protective of Diane and a bit cynical if you ask me. But she is kind and nice to me and lets me spend the night when my mother doesn't pick me up—like tonight for instance.

Diane and I have a lot of fun wrapping our gifts for our mothers. I bought mine a green blouse—her favorite style, her favorite color. I even wrap it in green paper and plop a big green bow on top. I worked a few hours every day after school at Carmen's Photo Studio to earn the money for it. Carmen does all the school photos for the yearbooks, so there's a lot of work there. Seventy-five cents an hour.

Diane and I stay up late laughing and talking, eating potato chips and drinking Coke. I sleep on the couch and around seven o'clock Sunday morning, my mother and some guy pull up in front of Diane's house and blow the horn. I pull the drapes back and wave to let them know I'll be right out. I see my mother lean over and hit the horn again.

I rush out to the car and get in the back seat. I hold the gift box in my lap. My mother hasn't noticed it yet. I don't know the guy driving, but I know they are both drunk. I wait a few minutes until we're about a block from Diane's and I can't wait any longer.

"Happy Mother's Day!"

I lean over the seat and hand my mother the gift. I kiss her cheek.

She holds the gift for a while. She stares at it, but says

nothing. I am so excited.

"Open it. Go ahead," I tell her.

She rolls down the window and tosses the unopened package out the window. She rolls the window back up.

We drive on.

That night after my mother and her new friend—who turns out to be a nice guy named Peyton—go out, I call and ask Diane how her mother liked the gift, the blue blouse.

"She liked it a lot. She put it on and it fit great. How about yours?"

"She loves hers, too."

Chapter 15

C. Peyton Williams III

My mother and I still live alone. She sees Leonard sometimes, but she spends her drinking time with Peyton.

Bobby is still with his dad in Sacramento, and Darryl lives down on Tallmadge Parkway with his dad.

I don't know how she managed it, but my mother found Peyton—a very rich drinking buddy who doesn't even move in with us. He helps my mother find a little-bit-nicer-than-we've-been-used-to apartment and loans her the money for one month's rent in advance. We now live on Adams Street near my school, the City Hospital, my Uncle Paul's bar, and a small grocery store. It's a fourth-floor walk-up. But we have a tiny balcony and a fake fireplace.

Peyton, whose full name is C. Peyton Williams III, is trying to escape his overly-protective parents. He's not a kid, he's my mother's age, but because Peyton is so rich, his whole family is worried that he will be taken advantage of by people like my mother and me. They do not understand Peyton's drinking problem. They think he's just trying to get back at them for something. They've blocked his accounts but he still gets what he refers to as maintenance. He always laughs after he says the word, "maintenance."

I like Peyton.

He and my mother drink too much to be lovers, yet he always makes sure she gets home safely even if it is in the early morning hours. He's a really good friend and drinking buddy, something my mother has never had in her life.

Usually he passes out on the couch with all of his clothes on. The only parts of his body I've seen are his arms. Most of the time he is gone when I get up for school in the morning. Occasionally, he is still on the couch. Then it's my job to wake him and give him a cup of steaming hot coffee before I leave for school. He spends his days in the local bars. I think he goes to his parents' house to shower and clean up about once a week or so. They live in a mansion. He carries a picture of it.

The neighbors on Adams Street hate us from day one. My mother and Peyton are oblivious to the disapproving stares and unaware of how loud they are at four o'clock in the morning, when they stagger upstairs. Peyton likes to sing old songs and he has a voice like a toad. Peyton is just plain loud. Drunk or sober. He is almost always gone by the time I get up for school in the morning.

Then late one night, I am snatched out of a nightmare by a loud noise in the living room, like the sound of a body being dropped from the ceiling. My bedroom is right next to the living room, so I can hear even a sock drop.

I open the door of my Pepto-Bismol pink bedroom and see Peyton passed out on the couch as usual.

But on the other side of the room, near the fake fireplace, my mother lies in a pool of blood. I rush to her, kneel down next to her, and see that all the blood is coming from one nasty gash over her right eyebrow. She is barely conscious.

I get close to her ear and whisper, "Mother."

No response.

I try waking Peyton, but he is too far gone to know who I am or what I want. He just hands me the keys to his car and waves me away.

I squeeze his hand and scream, "Peyton, wake up! I can't drive your car."

He snorts loudly, turns his back to me, as if nothing is wrong. I don't know exactly what to do. The puddle of dark red blood looks like an oil leak under an old car. I grab a towel and throw it into the pool of blood to soak it up. Then I get a second towel and wrap it around my mother's head like a turban, covering the gash as best I can.

I put Peyton's car keys into my pocket, and coax and drag my mother to the door. Somehow we get down the four flights to the street, but not without the neighbors seeing and hearing us. Thank god, the car is parked right out front.

I hold her up against the fender while I unlock the car. Then I push and pull and beg until she is lying down in the back seat. When I slam the door, she returns to her blackout, mumbling, "What the hell is this? I'm all sticky!"

I climb into the driver's seat. Peyton is tall and I have never driven before and I can't figure out how to move the seat up. I can't believe I am going to drive a brand new black Mercedes either. I have no choice and besides I can practically see the hospital from in front of our apartment building.

I drive in one gear. At a red light that seems to last forever, a random memory snatches my brain.

Random Memory

I was five years old and pretending to ice skate up in my grandmother's bathroom after a bath. I slid around in the puddles of water, the mess I had made. I slipped and tried to grab the edge of the white porcelain sink, but it caught my chin instead. The next thing I knew I was in the back seat of a yellow cab and my mother was holding me. I was still naked, but she had wrapped me in a blanket. She held a towel under my chin. I remember the warmth and the blood and the love. She was frightened for me. Now I'm frightened for her.

I touch my chin and feel the scar from so long ago.

Back to Real Life

The light changes to green and we continue jerking our way up to the emergency entrance of City Hospital, where I get out and yell through the open doors.

"Please help us!"

An attendant comes out and motions to someone inside to get a gurney.

My mother is only slightly resistant and they are able to get her onto the stretcher. The attendant takes off the blood-soaked turban. There is still so much blood. My mother looks even tinier than she really is, like an innocent wounded child.

"Who the hell are you? Get your fucking hands off me," she yells to the attendant.

No one notices that I am the driver, that I am a kid, or that I have blood all over me, too. They get her inside and into a room where they clean her up, and give her a local anesthetic. The bleeding stops almost immediately, even though she is not paying any attention to their instructions.

"Honey. Hold her hand or something. She'll be more comfortable if she can see you," the attendant says to me.

I take her hand in mine. There is dried blood all over her heart-shaped ring, the one Ardith hocked to her. The two little diamond chips look like rubies. There is caked blood between her fingers, and under her nails. I kiss her hand and the smell of dried blood makes me a little queasy.

"This is your mother, right?" the attendant asks. "Has she been drinking tonight?"

At first I think he is kidding. But he is not, so I nod. One stitch and she is struck suddenly and completely sober. She pulls her hand away from me, and looks right into my eyes.

"Isn't this a school night, honey?" she slurs.

The attendant cuts away from the one stitch. Before he can start the second stitch, she is on her feet, out of the room and marathon running down the corridor to the exit.

"Catch her!" I yell to the attendant

But he tells me to let her go.

The other attendant cuts me with his words, "She's just a drunk."

I pretend not to hear him and tears come to my eyes as I try to catch up with her. She is faster than I am and had a head start. Besides, I take the time to apologize to everybody I see on the way out. I stop and watch her open the door and enter my uncle Paul's bar. It's just across the street from the hospital.

The security guard yells for me to get the Mercedes out of the way, even though I am obviously not old enough to drive. I drive home in the one gear I know.

I have to ignore the blood on the stairs at home because I am in such a hurry to get into the apartment and call Uncle Paul. When I reach him he promises me he will bring her home when he closes the bar. I trust him to do that.

At home Peyton is still snoring on the couch. He has wet himself and smells really bad.

I clean up as much blood as I can before going to bed. Just before falling asleep, I think about my friend Diane and how jealous she will be when I tell her I drove a Mercedes.

I wish I had a dog.

Chapter 16

At Long Last High School

We still live on Adams Street—the longest we've lived anywhere—and I'm a freshman at Central High School. All I want to do is get good grades and make a few friends.

The good grades come easily, but making new friends takes a long time.

Then on the very first day of my sophomore year, I fall in love with a new arrival named Jim, a Lutheran over-achiever from a normal home. He gets high grades, plays all sports, and walks on water. When I ask what color his eyes are, he says, "rapture blue."

His ego is bigger than Cleveland. He likes me, so I become his girlfriend. We go steady, which just means we make out a lot in the front seat of his sister's white Valiant. The windows get foggy, but kissing and holding each other tightly is as far as it goes.

We break up for a while in our junior year because I get angry when he makes out with a girl named Judy at a party I wasn't invited to. Judy tells everyone about it and everyone tells me. I walk around singing one of my favorite songs. *"Now it's Judy's turn to cry, Judy's turn to cry."* There seems to be a lot of songs on the radio about crying and parties. There is another one I like. *"It's my party and I'll cry if I want to, die if I want to."* I make a promise to myself. I'm not getting married—ever.

Out of the Car

It is a big thing to me this falling out of a friend's car. I am in the backseat with Diane and a couple of other girls and it is raining buckets. We are on our way home from the Friday night football game out at the Rubber Bowl. Central versus Garfield. We won and are on our way to celebrate at the Waterloo Drive-in where they have the best hamburgers, French fries, and onion rings in the world. Chocolate milkshakes to die for.

On Arlington Street, not far from the Rubber Bowl, I lean a little too hard on the back door and fall out into the street, face first into the rain, into the oncoming traffic. My friend who is driving goes into shock. Her car spins around in front of me and another car, a dark green one, crisscrosses it. I land in a kneeling, upright, prayer position. I open my eyes and see how close the two cars are.

If I had fallen flat out I would have been crushed by both cars. The paramedics arrive to take me to the hospital, but I refuse to ride with them. I want to get back into the car I was in. I am probably in shock too, so the paramedics follow behind our car all the way to Children's Hospital. Both of my knees are now at the back of my legs. No blood. No cuts. Just a lot of pain.

Some of my friends and other curiosity seekers meet me at the hospital. My now ex-boyfriend, Jim, is with them. I hear someone yell, "She'll do anything for attention."

This is followed by a lot of laughter. I hear Jim's laugh above the rest.

My knees hurt. The doctors can do nothing without my mother's permission. She isn't at the View Lunch, Aunt Pat's, Grandma's, Joe's All-Stars, home. She is nowhere to be found.

I look up my Uncle Raymond's phone number in the Cuyahoga Falls phone book and call his house. Thankfully he is home and I beg him to help me. He speaks to the doctor and assumes full responsibility for whatever procedures need to be done. God bless Uncle Raymond. He's Mom's brother and Grandma's favorite.

All my friends, except Diane, and Jim, are long gone. It's after midnight.

The doctor relocates my knees or reconnects them or whatever it is they do to knees, bandages them and gives me crutches.

We all head out to the Waterloo in Jim's sister's Valiant to celebrate winning the game.

Chapter 17

Baby Michi's Baby

My baby cousin Michi is 15 years old and pregnant. Aunt Pat forbids an abortion because, as she says, "Catholics don't kill babies." She's not Catholic, but she was once married to one. Aunt Pat has had several abortions that even I know about.

She checks Michi into the Florence Crittenden Home for Unwed Mothers on East Market Street across the street from Eckard's Funeral Home and the Disabled American Veterans Club.

To me it looks like a prison, but it's a baby factory, a place for girls and women of all ages and backgrounds to give birth and then give their babies up for adoption. I feel sorry for Michi and grateful that it's not me. Of course it couldn't be me, I'm a virgin and imagine I always will be.

I'm old enough to drive now, so I borrow Mom's car and visit Michi on Sundays to take her out to Green Gables Restaurant for our favorite fried chicken, and then we just drive around anywhere to give her a change of scenery. Michi is beautiful and such a baby herself that I worry about her. She talks very matter-of-factly about the Crittenden Home and sits with her hands folded over her gigantic belly.

"I feel sorry for all those poor girls. Some of them are so sad. And most of them are really nice."

Michi is extremely kind and sensitive, but Aunt Pat has made my favorite cousin a little bit confused about life.

Michi names her baby and lets him go to a loving family. In my heart, I am grateful that this baby is getting a chance to have a real family. I think Michi feels the same way.

She goes right back to school, but when she turns 17, she falls in love with a boy named Tim and she is soon pregnant again. This time Aunt Pat keeps her at home.

Chapter 18

My Mother's Bottom

"Public drunkenness. You are a disgrace as a woman and a mother. And you are still drunk this morning, aren't you?"

"Goddamn right I am, your Honor."

My mother's angry voice fills the courtroom as she stands defiantly before the judge.

Her faithful Leonard has hung on through her increasingly out of control life. He and I sit on an old blonde wooden bench in the last row of the crowded courtroom. From where we are, my 39-year-old mother looks like a little girl. She's only five feet tall and her long curly auburn hair is pulled back into a thick ponytail.

The judge shakes his head, and tells her, "Your fine—this time—is 200 dollars and you will attend—*you will attend*—three Alcoholics Anonymous meetings within the next two weeks. You will pay the 200 dollars when you bring in your signed report cards attesting to the fact that you have attended the meetings.

"What if I just pay 300 and skip those damn meetings?"

"Then, my beautiful young woman, you will go to jail."

He pounds his gavel on the desk.

My disheveled mother, clad only in dirty pedal pushers, a flimsy green and blue plaid shirt and sandals, attempts the humbling walk to the back of the courtroom without staggering. She wobbles, but she finally reaches us. We have brought her jacket from home. Leonard holds it open for her. She pushes it away.

"Get away from me. I don't need your help. I need a drink and I'm dying for a cigarette. Let's go."

She focuses on me.

"And you—Goody Two-shoes—why aren't you in school?"

We walk up the block from the courthouse and cross Main Street to go into the nearest bar. Whitelaw's is a landmark downtown bar owned by a Jewish man who wanted my mother to let his wife and him adopt me several years ago. Mother gave him an emphatic no at the time and talked for a long time about, "The nerve… the nerve of that man."

This is a bar I like, too, because since I was six they've been serving me Shirley Temples, on the house, and they never forget that I hate maraschino cherries. This is also where my mother, Aunt Pat and Mom drink while I do their Christmas shopping for them at Polsky's and O'Neill's. Aunt Pat has charge accounts out the wazoo. In December, Whitelaw's is decorated for Christmas and smells of pine needles and spices and eggnog.

Leonard and I are starving, so we order and scoff down our hamburgers and cokes while Mother polishes off three drinks and is so polluted and exhausted from her night in jail that we are able to get her out of there, into the car and home to sleep it off, without too much effort and without the scene I was dreading.

The good news about Leonard is that he's not an alcoholic and he isn't aware of how dangerous our situation is. He drinks a little bit, just to be near my mother and to take care of her. He's a sponge for abuse, and he loves her, so I am not the only receptacle for her rage now.

My mother does not call AA or go to a meeting, even though Leonard and I both nag her about it. She drinks more and more and with a new vengeance. At least she drinks at home now, so I always know where she is.

One evening, someone pounds on our apartment door. When I open it slightly, I see a roundish gray-haired older man and a man and woman about my mother's age.

"We're friends of Bill's. AA. Alcoholics Anonymous. I'm Bill S. and my young friends here are Chick and Dottie," the older man smiles warmly and says.

I open the door when I hear that. Leonard is at work and my mother is in the kitchen drinking and trying to cook something that she calls Slumgoolian, which is actually macaroni, tomato soup, and ground chuck.

I let the three strangers in and take them into the kitchen.

"Who the hell are you?" my mother asks, with no restraint. "And what the hell are you doing in my kitchen?"

They introduce themselves.

"Someone from the courthouse called us. It is mandatory that you go to a meeting of Alcoholics Anonymous with us tonight."

My mother throws the pot she is stirring across the room. It hits the wall and most of the Slumgoolian lands on the floor.

She turns her back on all of us and stomps out of the kitchen. I start after her, but Chick takes my hand and Dottie follows my mother into her bedroom.

I'm nervous so I keep talking to pass the time. I tell Chick about my friend Suellen and how my mother cooked dinner for the three of us one night and it was this Slumgoolian just like she's fixing tonight. And that it was delicious.

In a remarkably short time, Dottie and my mother come out of her bedroom, and they all leave for an AA meeting at King School, a school I went to in the third grade when I lived with my Aunt Laura and Uncle Raymond. My mother is closed up like a clam, borderline drunk, and is resigned to going with them.

Still holding my hand, Chick says to me, "Don't worry. She's safe with us."

I am more worried about them than I am about her, but I can't say that.

When Chick and Bill bring her home around midnight, I am sitting in the now-clean kitchen eating some of the salvaged Slumgoolian and finishing my homework.

"We dropped my wife off at home," Chick tells me. "She had about all the abuse she could stand for one night."

I take a really close look at my mother. Her skin is yellow, she probably weighs less than 90 pounds, and she sits at our kitchen table hurling insults at two sober men. She begs for a drink. There is not a drop left in our apartment and it is Sunday. Ohio still has a blue law—no alcohol sold on Sundays. My mother begins taunting them.

"You're not real men. You're afraid to take even one drink," she says.

It turns out, Chick has a friend who owns a bar and he sends Bill to pick up a bottle of Seagram's Seven Crown. Once she knows the booze is on its way, she calms down a little. Bill returns soon enough and she goes back into the bottle.

I am grateful for that because she is coming on to Chick in a big way right in front of me, and I am not sure what will happen next. Chick tries talking to me to avoid her.

"I've got two sons about your age," he tells me. "They've put up with a lot of bunk with Dottie and me."

"How old are they?" I ask.

"Rob's 14 and Chuck's 15."

"I'm 16."

At about three in the morning, Chick and Bill are tired and ready to go home.

Chick looks me right in the eye again and says, "You should be grateful just to be alive. You know that, don't you? And, don't you worry we're not giving up on her. We will be back tomorrow night about the same time."

After Chick and Bill leave, my mother gazes coldly at me and mumbles, "Miss Goody Two-shoes."

Leaving her alone at the table, I go to my room and thank god for Chick and Dottie and Bill and AA. I wonder if Chick and Dottie's sons are as weird as I am.

My mother continues to drink a little while longer, but from that night on, her drinking is never quite the same. Her heart isn't in it. She is home in bed most of the time and growing unhappier by the day.

Leonard moves in with us, which is good timing for me. In one month I will graduate from high school and I need time to study for exams.

Shiekie Meets Leonard

It is June of 1963, and my dad flies in from New York to celebrate my high school graduation with us. He is charming, entertaining, and funny and at night my mother, in her drunkenness crawls into bed with him, even though Leonard is only one room away.

The next morning, my mother is too hung over to attend my graduation. Dad and Leonard sit together like old friends and smile throughout the ceremony. I get a few awards and a small scholarship from the Akron Women's City Club. It makes me happy to see them out there in the audience, and every time I walk across the stage, they applaud.

Dad and I make our plans for two of my girlfriends—Diane and Joanne—and me to spend the summer with him, and he returns to New York the next day. I keep waiting for him to say something about my mother and what's going on with the drinking, but he doesn't. Not a word. And then he's gone.

The Party's Over
A week and a half later, on a beautiful June night, when my mother has drunk herself nearly dead, she goes into convulsions. I call an ambulance. I call Chick and Dottie and Bill from AA. They all arrive about the same time and she is taken to St. Vincent's Hospital, the only place in Akron that has an alcohol treatment program that admits women. Nuns run it.

The rehabilitation program generally lasts 28 days. They are keeping my mother 70 days. She is suffering from malnutrition and pneumonia, as well, and needs more than just treatment for alcohol dependency.

Summer
Diane, Joanne and I go to New York as planned. I am secure in the fact that my mother is safe in the hospital. All three of us girls stay with my dad in his tiny Brighton Beach apartment. Betty is still in Seagate with the kids, so presumably my dad lives alone. But he has a girlfriend, married of course, who hangs around all the time. Harriet is a Jewish Princess, who absolutely loves and is actually obsessed with my dad. I ask him what it is about her that he likes so much.

"Are you blind? Did you get a good look at her body?" he replies.

I promise myself that I will never ask him another question about Harriet. My friends and I giggle half the night about his answer.

Harriet tries, I'll give her that. She cooks for all of us even though she is in the midst of redecorating and cleaning the apartment. Her favorite color is orange and she loves leopard patterns. My friends and I are cutting in on her time and she hates it, especially when Dad takes us all to see "Camelot," then to dinner at her favorite Chinese restaurant.

As we have been planning for months, Diane, Joanne and I go into the city to buy tickets to see our idol, Paul Newman, in a new play called "Baby, Want a Kiss?" We are so happy with those tickets. The show is scheduled to open on Friday night. The night before we have to return to Akron.

On opening night, the three of us get all dressed up and take the D train to 42nd Street and Sixth Avenue. We practically float over to the Music Box Theatre on the *Great White Way*.

The large sign out front reads. "Opening Postponed."

We go inside. I step up to the window, tickets in hand.

"May I see the manager, please?" I ask one of the staff.

"No, you may not. We will be happy to exchange your tickets for you."

"I want to see the manager." I continue.

When I will not leave and have embarrassed my friends so much that they are half a block away, the stage manager comes out and asks me what my problem is. I rattle on about our dilemma.

"I am sorry, but all we can do is exchange your tickets for next week." He says.

"Do you have a match?" I ask.

"You're too young to smoke."

"I don't smoke. I want to set you on fire."

He makes me leave the theatre. But before I will go, I write a note to Paul Newman about our disappointment.

A few weeks after we get back to Akron, he replies to my note and sends a signed program.

But for now the three of us are so depressed that we head over to the Beacon Hotel bar where my dad works to tell him our sad story. We arrive at Broadway and 75th at the precise moment my father is tossing an angry customer through the bar's plate glass window.

Chapter 19

New Life

When I get home from my summer in New York, everything is completely different. Leonard bought a house on Lurie Avenue, way across town from Mother's usual hangouts, and he has moved all our stuff into it. He apologizes because it's small. I force myself not to cry. This is the nicest place my mother and I have ever lived. He shows me around our new home and tells me that he and my mother are getting married. Leonard gives me the best news last.

"In a few weeks, we're going to get your brother Darryl back from his father."

Mother's coming home today. I am terrified. I grew up in her blackouts and I am afraid she won't even know who I am. Leonard scares me without meaning to when he tells me that I probably won't even know her and that she is completely different. I wait at the new house while Leonard picks her up from the hospital.

When I hear Leonard's old pink and gray DeSoto pull up outside, I take a deep breath and close my eyes before I open the front door. He motions for me to come out to the car to help carry some things. My mother holds a small plant, a purple African violet in a clay pot. Leonard hands me a couple of shopping bags full of clothes. He carries the suitcase.

It's a little chilly out even though it is only mid-September. The air is crisp and it hurts a little when I breathe it in.

Mother says nothing at all about the new house, and puts the violet down on an end table and walks over to me. She stands in front of me with her eyes downcast. I put my arms around her, pull her to me, and hold her tightly. She lets her arms dangle at her sides, but she doesn't push me away. I kiss her on the cheek before she backs away.

"I love you, Mother."

She whispers her question softly, "Do you?"

And then she goes straight upstairs to lie down.

Leonard yells from the kitchen, "I'll fix some coffee, hon."

I sit in the unfamiliar kitchen at the new yellow and gray

Formica table and watch Leonard open a packet of Sanka instant coffee.

We are both quiet a long while before he asks me if I think she is all right.

I say the first thing that comes to my mind.

"She looks healthier."

Leonard confesses that he doesn't know what to do next.

"She still needs to get Vitamin B shots and the hospital recommended a psychiatrist, a Dr. Dove Roman."

I ask him about AA and her three saviors.

"I guess that's pretty much for the rest of her life. I can't say I understand it myself, but they visited her at the hospital every single day."

The attic is mine, so I tiptoe past their bedroom and up the stairs to my new sanctuary. I pray that she will be all right.

It's so quiet now that she's sober.

The Other Shoe

Every night she attends an AA meeting with Bill and Chick and Dottie.

I am in my freshman year at Akron University and work part-time at WSLR, a country/western radio station, writing commercial copy, doing on-air sketches, and secretarial work for the General Manager.

I do not know the stranger who is my mother. She does not know me. I am proud of her and happy to see her sticking to something that is so difficult. I understand that AA is a miracle for us. At the encouragement of her new AA friends, she takes classes—typing and shorthand. She is the best in her shorthand class.

I overhear her asking Leonard one night, "What good is it if I can take shorthand really, really fast, if I can't type it up?"

During that first year of sobriety, there is an enormous AA Conference held in Akron, which is the birthplace of Alcoholics Anonymous. Mother invites me to go. I am a nervous wreck. She is a nervous wreck. We go anyway with Bill and Chick and Dottie. Leonard has to work.

There are hundreds of people seated around tables of 10 or so drinking coffee and smoking cigarettes, laughing and having a good time without alcohol.

One of the founding members of AA is on the podium, along with a lot of other really nice looking sober people. I count at least 20 priests and a lot of nuns in their black-and-white habits. I make jokes in my head about it looking like a visit to the zoo to see the penguins, and I also fantasize about pouring just a little bit of vodka into everyone's water glass.

Then the stories begin. Although each one is more horrifying than the one before, not one can hold a candle to my mother's. Not that she would ever tell her story to anyone. They all seem to glow with an inner calmness and serenity. My mother's smile is pasted on and does not change. But I know that today my mother is truly happy. I have never seen her this way. I love her and am so proud of her. She is so beautiful and so frightened.

Life gets better and Darryl does come back to live with us. I feel like a jigsaw puzzle that had a piece missing and now I feel whole again.

About a month later, my mother is asked to read aloud from the Big Book of Alcoholics Anonymous at one of their nightly meetings.

"Put on your glasses," someone yells from the audience. And people laugh.

She does not wear glasses. She didn't even know she needed them until this moment. She is so embarrassed that she leaves the meeting and never returns to AA. She never drinks again, but her fear of people keeps her from ever going to another AA meeting. Bill, Chick and Dottie beg, but she tells them, "I can't go back. I can't. I just can't."

I have always liked school, but I do not want to live at home and go to Akron University, an engineering school. I want to go to Kent State and major in journalism, but the scholarship I received is for Akron University, only.

So I am at the school I did not choose, working in the basement of the Admissions Office, typing letters to other students who have been chosen to attend the school. I also type the rejections. All this to earn money for books for courses I think will lead me nowhere.

Chapter 20

Trouble

Is there anything more to tell about Shiekie? About my dad?

- He's proud
- Feelings are easily hurt
- Narcissistic
- Intelligent
- Talented
- Gambler
- Handsome ladies' man
- Man's man
- People want to be like him
- He never contemplates suicide, only murder
- He is never wrong
- He thinks like a thief

Most importantly, Shiekie now has a medium-sized generic brown dog named Trouble that lives with him in the apartment on Brighton Fourth Street in Brooklyn. He is my dad's constant companion after Betty leaves and takes the kids. And after his girlfriend Harriet dies at a young age. And after one girlfriend gives him the kiss-off. And after another girlfriend moves to Trump City, way out in the Bronx.

Trouble loves my dad. Dad is his best friend. He trains Trouble to hate the people he hates. And he drives the dog a little crazy by pretending to hold a parakeet in his hands and talking to his hands the way he used to when they really did have a parakeet, before Trouble ate him. Dad doesn't let on to Trouble that the parakeet is never coming back. Whenever I visit, I call first to let Dad know I am on my way so he can lock Trouble in the bedroom. I am afraid of him because Dad always warns me, "The dog's sick. Mad. He'll bite your face off if you get near him. I don't know what's wrong with him."

I like dogs, but this is a warning I cannot ignore.

My dad loves it when Zaydeh comes to the door because Trouble really doesn't like him and he'll bark and bark and snarl and growl and show his teeth. So says my dad. I guess

Zaydeh used to just walk into the apartment anytime he wanted. The door is never locked.

"Now I don't have to listen to Pop's crap every day—about all the things he's done for me," he says.

Only Dad can walk Trouble and only with a muzzle on the dog, to be on the safe side. This he does faithfully. He loves that the neighborhood yentas cross the street when they see him and Trouble coming.

One weekend I visit and while we are out to dinner, someone tries to break into the apartment. Dad's apartment is on the first floor facing the back alley so it is easily accessible, but because everyone knows about Trouble, no one bothers. Dad never worries about it.

Then some bozo climbed up the fire escape, cut through the screen and Trouble let him have it. Dad shows me the bloody pieces of shirt and what looks like the tip of somebody's finger.

I hear him in the bedroom later.

"Good Trouble. Good Trouble. Who's a good boy?"

One time I forget to call for some silly reason and I knock on the door. Trouble is loose in the apartment. I knock some more. No answer. Just the barking.

Well, the door isn't locked, and I push it open a little. Trouble pushes through the opening, knocks me down and licks my face. He and I go back inside, where he finds his red ball and brings it to me. I throw it for him.

No Dad.

So Trouble and I get on Dad's bed to watch television and wait. The dog is all over me, bringing me toys, licking me, rolling on his back for a good scratch and wagging his tail. We are curled up together and half asleep when Dad comes home.

Trouble barks at my dad. My poor dad shouts at him.

"Shut up you traitor, you mangy mutt."

Chapter 21

Stepfather Three—Husband Five

Leonard is not so handsome as I remember him, but he is oddly interesting looking. He has a catalogue of annoying habits: snorting, picking his nose, mispronouncing words. He says "Eye-talian" and he's Italian. He says "sWordfish." He repeats every word spoken to him by someone else as if he is saying—and we're hearing—the words for the first time. He likes flashy clothes and jewelry and *Aramis* cologne. He loves spaghetti with any sauce and he slurps his very hot coffee with cream and sugar. He has a drink now and then, usually a glass of Chianti. I love him for his kindness, generosity and for loving us.

Leonard also saved my mother's life, my life and my brother Darryl's life. He treats us better than we treat him most of the time, but he knows how much we care about him.

He works at Goodyear Tire & Rubber Company, where he has worked all of his adult life. Once he was put on probation for devoting too much time to my mother and not enough to his work. Later Goodyear promoted him to supervisor and he was so happy. His wish was to always work hard and to live well.

He doesn't care much for Aunt Pat or Mom and they act as if he doesn't exist most of the time. If they want something, of course, he is the first person they call.

He is a great man. He loves my mother. He gets her psychotic family in the bargain. We are no bargain.

After I move to New York, he looks forward to my holiday visits because I talk to him like he's another human being. I even start to listen when he repeats what I say. I am not the loving daughter all the time, but I try.

He spends his spare time gardening and grows magnificent roses. He makes friends with all their neighbors in Fairlawn where he and Mother bought the home of their dreams—or at least close to it. He mows the lawn every other day so that it looks just right.

My mother stops going outside, little by little. First

she stops going into the backyard or out on the patio. She also waits until dark before she backs her car out of the garage and down the driveway to the mailbox to pick up the mail and *The Akron Beacon Journal.*

"I don't want the damned, nosy neighbors watching every move I make."

Part II

Chapter 22

Prince Harming 1969

I'm an adult now, whatever that means. I'm married and everything and have done all the things I swore I'd never do. At this precise moment, I am lying on the ground outside my house, face down in the dirty New Jersey snow.

When we were kids back in Ohio, my cousins and I made angels in the pure white snow. And when my mother was seven months pregnant with Bobby in 1955, she almost miscarried when she fell backwards into a snowdrift outside some bar. And I will never forget all that damn snow in Nevada on the way to Sacramento. I hate snow.

Yet here I am, alone in the snow with the dog I always wanted. My huge German Shepherd, Chance, licks my face, my neck, my ears, my eyes. He wants me to get up. I'd like to stand up, but as I am a failure at shoveling just six inches of new snow from the driveway so I can get our almost brand new 1968 Volkswagen bug out and be on time for visiting hours at Hackensack Psychiatric, I'd rather just lie here and freeze.

I don't feel like going to the hospital to visit my husband today, anyway. I want to lie here in the snow until I die. I want to feel the warmth that's rumored to come with freezing. I want to be *The Little Match Girl.*

A concerned neighbor stops outside my gate and stomps his feet to get the snow off his boots.

"Aren't you cold?" he asks.

"No. I'm fine. Just resting," I say as I lift my head and smile.

I want the neighbor to disappear.

"Saw the ambulance at your place the other night," he says. "Everything OK?"

Chance barks and bares his teeth as he lunges at the man on the other side of the chain link fence. I ignore him and wait to hear the Good Samaritan's footsteps as he walks away. Shit, if they're going to badger me, I might as well get up.

With each heavy shovelful of ice and snow I try to understand how I ended up living in a corner house on half an acre in Saddle Brook, New Jersey, with a German Shepherd named Chance and a husband named John John, who just happens to be in the loony bin.

And Then It All Comes Back to Me

I keep on shoveling as I remember. I left my sober Mother and Akron University to move to New York to study at The American Academy of Dramatic Arts. And, of course, I was searching for love and maybe a little bit of sanity. And then it all comes back to me. I remember too much now.

How I Met John John in 1967

I am running from the American Academy of Dramatic Arts on 21st Street and Madison to my apartment on 24th and Second. I am excited because I just got the lead in the 1967 summer production of *South Pacific*. I don't know how I got it. I can't sing; I can't dance. I used Happy Birthday as my audition piece. For some reason, the director, Harry Mastrogeorge, chose me to play Nellie Forbush—the lead. This is my happiest day. I am an actress.

When I reach my building, I give my favorite doorman a hug, decide not to wait for the elevator, and run up the nine flights to the apartment I share with my friend Arlene and her cousin. I could never afford this great apartment alone.

The door is unlocked. I push it open with my foot.

From the doorway of my apartment, I see the most beautiful creature on Earth. A boy who looks like an angel sits on my bed holding an 8x10 black-and-white glossy photo of me, and he's smiling. His teeth are so perfect and so white that I wonder if they are real. His guitar rests against my bed.

"Hello?"

"Hello, Lovely," he says. "I'm John John. Will you marry me?"

"I'm never getting married and you're way too beautiful," I reply.

I am not afraid. Oh, not at all afraid of this person. I close the door and lock it. I sit on the bed near him, putting my gray canvas bag between us.

"Don't you want to know where your flatmate is?" My angel asks.

"Sort of," I reply.

"I just met her, too," he tells me. "She and my best friend have gone to get a bite. I think he wants to sell her an insurance policy. Your other flatmate is working late. Hungry, Love?"

"Are you real?" I ask him.

He touches my arm and a jolt of electricity runs through my body and soul and sticks like a thorn in my heart. I stuff some money in my jeans pocket and lead him and his guitar out of the apartment. In the elevator mirror, he stares at me. I stare back.

He slings the guitar over the shoulder of his custom-made multi-colored velvet jacket. His bell-bottoms are just the right too tight. And boots. And boots. Hand-stitched. He pushes his long, straight blondish-brownish hair back from his face with his perfect hands. I could eat his chocolate eyes.

Thud. The elevator stops. We stare at each other until the doors try to close again and he opens them with a thrust of his perfect arm.

Still Shoveling That New Jersey Snow

Thud. Another shovelful of snow. With that jolly summer memory of the first time I met JJ, my husband, stuck in my brain, I realize that I've shoveled at least enough to get the car out of the garage. Chance squats and sprays the snow yellow all around him. He's a 160-pound male dog and he squats. What have I done to him?

"Good boy. Good pee. Let's go."

I know I'm late for visiting hours, but I'm cold and I want hot coffee and a drink. So I sit on the kitchen floor and have another cup of coffee with a little bit of Grand Marnier as a chaser. Chance puts his head in my lap. He's as wet as I am and smells of dog. Chance licks the Grand Marnier from my lips. He loves Grand Marnier, too.

Memories

Where was I? Oh. Yes. John John is very real. The doorman acknowledges both of us when I trip over my feet right outside my apartment building. I'm embarrassed, apologetic.

"I'm always tripping."

"Me, too," JJ says.

Then he giggles. It's a most unusual giggle. We walk and talk until sunset. We forget all about dinner and go to the roof of my building and wait for darkness when lights like giant candles go on in skyscrapers all over the city.

"I'm afraid of heights."

"Me, too," he says.

We sit on a metal box so close to each other that I am afraid we will be glued together when we stand up. He takes off his coat of many colors and puts it around my shoulders. It smells of expensive cologne and him. He notices that I'm sniffing his cologne.

"*Vetivert.*"

I ask where he lives.

"You mean, now?"

I nod.

"London, love. Hampstead, actually. I'm visiting my family in Newark. I was born in Russia. They came here and sent me to England."

"When?"

"I was 14. They sold me to the guy I live with. Lionel Bart."

"You live with a man? You live with Lionel Bart? The Lionel Bart who wrote *Oliver?* How do you mean live? What do you mean, they sold you?"

"We're lovers, sort of. But now I know I have always been looking for you."

"Won't this Bart guy get angry if you leave?"

"Yes, Lovely. He will."

"JJ, what do you do in London besides live?"

"Singer, actor, songwriter, musician. I've just finished doing the Artful Dodger in *Oliver* in the East End. I wrote the theme song for *The Russians Are Coming, The Russians Are Coming.*"

"The movie? With Alan Arkin?" I ask.

My prince smiles and kisses my lips, my eyes, my cheeks. I'm tingling. I've never felt a touch like his. I search for what I am feeling. New feelings. I feel warmth, maybe joy, maybe love. Safe. That's it. I feel safe and I want to cry.

Back to Reality in New Jersey

Chance licks my lips again and I am back in real time. I get up and put the coffee cup into the dishwasher.

"Chance. You stay here, sweetheart. You have to guard the house."

The present like the past is way too painful for me today, so on the drive to Hackensack via Route 4, I force my thoughts back again to that first encounter with JJ. Today doesn't seem real to me, so I let my mind take me back those two years.

Love on the Roof

The day we met in 1967 is so vivid to me. Wish today were as clear.

I remember that we stay on that rooftop until two a.m. My roommates are home now. His friend has gone back to Jersey.

My apartment building is new, so the model apartments are still functional. I rehearse with friends in them sometimes. I take him to an open one. We are like orphans in a very Grimm Fairy Tale. Fully clothed and laughing at ourselves, we climb onto the cardboard bed and cuddle and kiss and talk and eventually fall asleep after swapping childhood horror stories and our dreams of fame and fortune.

I wake up from time to time to find him staring at me and playing his guitar. Sometimes singing something that sounds like a lullaby.

In the morning, I call in sick for work at Twentieth-Century Fox where I am the number three secretary in the Foreign Department for David Raphel. I also audition with other actors for the Casting Director, Alixe Gordon. She calls me when someone like Jeff or Beau Bridges or Martin Sheen comes in and they can't come up with an actress to read opposite them. They've told me I'm good, but they always hire someone else. I'm not even considered human. Just a warm body. Sometimes I do stunts for Fox, too. Today I will be sick for them.

"I love you, JJ."

"Do you?" He smiles.

"My mother always says that when I tell her I love her."

"And I love you, too, Lovely."

We make plans. Plans.

I have never had sex with a man or a woman. He has never had sex with a woman. We're a little confused in that area so we decide to wait a while to consummate. Touching is plenty for us for now.

Lionel

The first night after JJ and I meet, I go into rehearsal for *South Pacific* at the Academy and he gets on a plane back to England to tell Bart it's over between them and he's leaving him for me.

The second night after JJ and I meet, I get a phone call from Bart.

"Listen you little twit, sod off."

Bart takes JJ to Portofino on holiday and I finish *South Pacific* and get a job on the road with a non-equity dinner theatre production of a mediocre Broadway play entitled *Paisley Convertible.* At least it's the lead. The director, Ken Eulo, casts me because I look like the innocent waif the script calls for. A newlywed in Manhattan.

The best thing about the play is that I meet Patty Pratt. She plays my mother even though she's three months younger than I am. She's from Oklahoma and she's a hoot. We have great times together in Greensboro, Nashville, Dallas, Fort Worth, Scottsdale. We laugh and drink our way through the south and southwest.

JJ writes to me every day from wherever he is. Long letters. Lyrics. Poems. After his holiday, he moves to New York and waits for me to return from the road.

Bliss

JJ and I are married on July 25, 1968, in the township of Monroe, in Michigan, by Joanne Nichols, Justice of the Peace. His parents disapprove so we find a state closest to New York that will marry a woman of 22 and a man of 20. It is an obscure Jewish holiday so to my father's chagrin, not even a reformed rabbi will perform the ceremony.

My mother and Leonard arrange a surprise wedding reception for us at the Holiday Inn in Akron. Aunt Pat is the catering manager there and she is sober and married to a very tall pianist. Michael, Michi, their spouses, my friend Susan from the Academy, my dad, and even Chick and Dottie and their sons I've never met, Rob and Chuck, are here for the big event. Darryl is 12 now and the best brother I can imagine. He giggles and asks me. "Did you bring your pajamas?"

We have a good time even though I don't drink that night, my wedding night, because I want to remember it all.

Hackensack

Less than two years after our wedding bliss, here I am in front of the Hackensack Psychiatric Hospital. I have too much junk in the car to carry by myself, but there's no one around to help. It'll take a few trips.

On my fifth trip into the hospital from the car, an orderly helps me carry the last of JJ's gear into his room.

JJ sits on a twin bed. He wears a hospital gown and no underwear. There are five people in the room with him, three women and two men, all dressed like JJ.

"Come in, Lovely. You brought my guitar."

I hand it to him and he throws me a kiss before he starts strumming and singing to his new audience. New fans for *"Mommy or Daddy or Baby, Which Do You Wish Me to Be?"*—the song he wrote for me. My favorite of all his songs.

While the orderly drags in his heavy amplifier, synthesizer and other stereo equipment, I back quietly out of the room.

Chapter 23

As Luck Would Have It

Prelude

Before Jersey, before Hackensack Hospital, before hell, in September of 1968, JJ and I are typical Manhattan newlyweds living in a second-floor walkup on 83rd Street between York and East End. We have over-sized furniture from Sloane's and a puppy that we name Chance.

One glorious autumn day while I am rushing to meet JJ, I catch sight of him as I round the corner at 57th and Sixth. I'm a few minutes late and he's waving frantically to make sure I see him. I smile and wave back.

The sky has been threatening rain all day and the downpour starts at that precise moment. JJ proudly opens our misshapen umbrella as he sprints across the Avenue against the light. We kiss and he clutches my hand as we run across to the other side. He is so wired that I think for a second that he's on amphetamines again.

He walks and talks so fast, I can hardly keep up with him in the pissing rain. I get sopping wet as I unsuccessfully try to stay under the umbrella with him.

Today's Audition

JJ talks on and on thinking I can hear him. He gestures and laughs out loud, but I am narcissistically reliving my own day while I stare at his beautiful head. His hair looks blonder today.

My day was hideous. I auditioned for *Butterflies Are Free* in a theatre in the East Village, along with a hundred other blondes. The director laughed out loud when he saw me.

"Are you nuts?" he said.

He shouted his comments across a lobby full of actors.

"You look like Keir Dullea's daughter. Get outta here."

Keir Dullea and Blythe Danner end up playing the leads.

After that humiliation, I treat myself to a drink at MacGregor's Garage. It's a Rusty Nail kind of day. Then I cram myself into the Seventh Avenue subway at rush hour. The rain melts taxis or the drivers go off duty out of spite. It's a New York City certainty.

Back to JJ's World

"Lovely, are you listening to me?"
"Where are we going, JJ?"
"A surprise, Lovely."
I stop. He stops.
"Lovely, we've hit the jackpot."
He pulls me closer to him under the umbrella. His *Vetivert*, the cologne we both wear now, smells so good in the rain. Huddled in a doorway on West 56th he blurts out his story.
"There I was minding my own business strolling across 56th Street to meet you. I was a little early for a change. And I see this bloke sneaking out of an alleyway between two buildings. I was close enough to see he had a gun in his right hand. He aims it at the backside of this older, heavyset sort of guy wearing a rain Mac."
I move in closer to hear better and to feel JJ's body heat.
"I run after the gun guy. He slips and falls, the gun goes off and the guy up ahead looks back at the one on the ground and then at me. Now, Lovely, here's the brilliant bit. The old bloke walks back to me, shakes my hand and kicks this other guy on the ground a little and picks up the gun and hands it to me. 'Hold on to this, will ya?'"
"You took the gun?"
"Yes, Lovely, I did."
"What about the guy on the ground?"
"He just lays there, head down. These guys know each other, Lovely. So the old guy says his name's Tony D. and this piss-ant's been bugging him for a while. Then he says he could sure use a guy like me."
"Where did he take you?"
"Just up the block here. That's where we're going. Tony wants to meet you."
"I want to go home, JJ. I want to feed Chance and see what part of the apartment he's eaten today. I don't feel like meeting some gangster."
"Tony D. is not a gangster. He gave me his card."
I squeeze JJ's hand and smile. I love him so much. But he

doesn't know from gangsters.

"Okay. Let's go meet your Don."

"And, Lovely, he's getting job-jobs for both of us. We'll have the same hours—four to midnight."

"You got me a job-job? We have jobs, remember. We're on a soap."

"Those aren't real jobs, Lovely. And they're not forever. Besides we always finish up by two, two-thirty in the afternoon. It's perfect. I told him all about us, that I'm a singer-songwriter and about Lionel Bart and you're an actress. He thinks I'm wonderful—honest, loyal, an asset—and he's going to absolutely adore you."

"You got us jobs from four to midnight doing what?"

"I'll tend bar at Tony's club and you'll be a room clerk at the Warwick Hotel where Cary Grant lives. Tony set it up with the General Manager."

"JJ—what about auditioning? We won't have any time."
"Lovely, we'll have the whole day. Are you ready for this? He's paying me a thousand a week plus tips and he says they'll be great because it makes people happy to see a good-looking guy like me behind the bar. He says you can come over every night after you leave work and we can cab it home together."

"So, do I get paid for my job or does this Tony think we come as a set?"

JJ kisses me gently on the top of my sopping wet head.

We walk on without speaking for a few minutes. Then he stops.

"Here we are, love."

We are in front of a nondescript two-story concrete building with blackened windows and no name, no sign, no identifying marks at all.

JJ holds the door open for me. I peer through the haze to see a gathering of gorgeous men lined up three thick around a curved bar. Rich, young, rich old; beautifully dressed men enjoying a happier hour than I ever have. Their voices are hushed.

We go all the way in, moving effortlessly through the crowd. I see the bartender staring at JJ and a few of the customers glancing his way, as well. Water drips off us, especially me, all the way up to the second floor via a winding staircase a la *Gone with the Wind*. The walls and carpets are dark blue. Someone good plays *"Sentimental Journey"* on the piano upstairs and the music floats out to us. My mother's favorite song.

At the top of the stairs to the left is a much larger and darker room with a grand piano and a larger and louder group of men. Everything and everyone looks some shade of purple. The sign outside the room on an easel reads. "Houston Allred at the piano."

JJ leads the way, and we turn right and enter Tony D.'s office. Tony does not stand to greet us. Instead he shouts and points.

"Shut the door. Sit."

And we do.

JJ's voice sounds far, far away and he is sitting right next to me. I try to remember if I have taken a Librium today. I hope I have some in my bag.

"My wife appreciates what you're doing for us, Tony. Don't you, Lovely?"

I cut JJ off and ask, "What exactly are you doing for us, Mr. D.?"

Tony smiles at me.

"Call me Tony. I hope you're not gonna give me a hard time after all the nice things JJ told me about you?"

I cock my head and stare at him defiantly.

"Your little woman's a smart aleck, JJ."

Tony leans as far across his desk as he can before his stomach gets in the way. He looks straight into my eyes.

"Please be as nice as you look. You're in for some good times if you let me help youse."

JJ holds my hand tightly—and just a little bit too tightly for my taste.

I take a deep breath.

"Of course, Tony. And I am happy JJ saved your life."

"Good. We understand each other. Good. I'm glad I'm alive, too."

Then he continues talking to JJ and I zone out.

The next thing I hear.

"Maybe you two need a little vacation before you start work."

JJ looks at me, then back at Tony before he says.

"Oh, no, Tony. You've done so much already."

"No, I haven't done nothing yet. I talked to my partner and he can put you two up in a suite for two weeks at the Americana in San Juan."

And then he hands JJ two first-class airline tickets—Pan Am.

"You'll leave tomorrow."

He unlocks a drawer in his desk, pulls out a wad of cash and shoves it toward JJ.

"Gimme back the gun, JJ."

JJ takes the frightening looking handgun out of his pocket and slides it over to Tony. Tony puts it into the nearest desk drawer and locks it.

The phone rings. Tony answers. JJ stuffs the money into my jacket pocket.

Tony holds his hand over the mouthpiece.

"Pack light. Now get outta here, the both of youse."

Tony manages to toss an air kiss and talk on the phone at the same time.

We leave the office and head for the smoke-filled purple room across the hall where we sit as close together in the comfortable booth as we can. I think JJ is excited by all of this.

The waiter is on us before we've made much of a dent in the posh velvet.

"What will the little lady have?"

"The little lady will have a scotch rocks. One rock. A double. Johnny Walker Black."

"What about you, gorgeous?" he asks JJ.

"And gorgeous will have a rum and coke." I answer for him.

I relax a bit and take a good long look around the room. Beautiful men hold hands, laugh, flirt, and make out—all the while looking like covers of *Esquire* and *GQ*.

The waiter is back with our drinks.

"Compliments of Mr. D.," he says.

"Tell Mr. D. we said thanks," JJ smiles his best smile

When the waiter floats away, I start.

"JJ, I don't trust Tony."

He kisses me gently on the lips and says, "Lovely, you don't trust anyone."

I see a couple of older men smiling at me when the

pianist starts to play *Secret Love.* JJ has half a drink left and I've already finished mine. I wave for the waiter as JJ puts his arm around me.

"Lovely, next time you see me in this room, I'll be the one at the piano singing a song I've written just for you. This is only the beginning."

JJ is happy. He examines the airline tickets over and over. He is excited about our trip to Puerto Rico. I kiss the palm of his hand.

"You know, it's just good timing that we aren't scheduled to work on the soap for the next three weeks. JJ, what's the name of this place?"

"The Candy Store."

All Expenses Paid

Puerto Rico, October 1968.

I hear a gentle tap on the door.

"Room Service, *señora*."

I wrap JJ's shirt around my naked body and cover my sleeping husband with the soft white sheet.

A young man rolls the room service cart into the room. Orange juice, yellow roses, breakfast, including a bottle of *Dom Perignon*. I offer a tip, but he backs away.

"Oh, no, no, no. It's all taken care of, *señora. Gracias.*"

There is no point in trying to wake JJ, so I roll the cart out onto the balcony and breathe in the clean ocean air. Our suite smells of hashish, leftover champagne and cigarettes, anyway.

I love the ocean. I rationalize that it is all right for us to be here as mafia guests while I drink hot black coffee and soak it all in. JJ did save Tony's life, after all. We never had a honeymoon. I will relax and enjoy this. JJ has traveled all over the world. I have been nowhere, seen nothing. I need this. Good coffee, but I can't eat yet. Too early.

My thoughts race back to my father and his gangster friends. I don't want to go there, so I go back into the room and take a couple of green and creamy white pills—Librium—before I lie down next to my sleeping husband.

When I awaken the second time, JJ is down by the pool in his baby-blue bathing suit—the one with the straps—that I bought him for his birthday. The browner he gets the better he looks. He instinctively turns, sees me standing on the balcony and waves. He has his guitar with him and a small crowd sits waiting for him to play. He motions for me to come down.

My brown-and-white checked bikini doesn't cover as much as I thought it would. I self-consciously wrap myself up in a large white hotel robe. The sauna and Jacuzzi help to heal my hangover and then I join JJ for a frozen daiquiri. He has made friends with a couple from Canada who have an ample supply of amphetamines and Quaaludes. They're on their honeymoon. JJ adores them already and I find that I like them, too.

Tony calls JJ or JJ calls Tony every day—at least twice.

"Guess what, Lovely, Tony wants us to come to his house for dinner the Sunday after we get home."

All I can think of is how much I don't like Tony and New Jersey, but I don't want to burst JJ's bubble, so I lie and tell him I think it's great, just great.

Late that night we wind our bodies together like spaghetti and although we fit together perfectly, sex for us is no walk in the park. JJ is gentle and tender but I don't think he knows how to make love. Since I've never been with anyone but him, I let him pound, bang and squish until he comes inside me, rolls over and smokes another joint or has another bit of hashish. I like hashish.

Some mornings after we've made love, I masturbate with the vibrating showerhead. While he sleeps I stare at his flaccid penis and think how ugly it is. The few penises I've seen before were circumcised. His looks like it's wearing a little hat. I love him, but I don't understand anything.

Honeymoon Over

We fly back to New York late on a Saturday night. Early Sunday morning a sleek black car with tinted windows shows up to take us to Tony's house in New Jersey. JJ and I are both hung over. On the way he takes speed while I try to sleep. Every once in a while I motion for the driver to roll down my window so I can vomit out onto the highway. Some of my vileness manages to cling to the door of the limo to humiliate me.

Tony's house is more of a compound than the mansion I'd imagined. Of course, his family is lovely: the wife, the son, the daughter, a perfect life. Bodyguards are everywhere, inside and outside the house. JJ and Tony leave me with the wife and daughter in the kitchen and go to the den to talk. In Tony's kitchen, I learn to tear lettuce properly.

On the way back to the city, JJ hands me an envelope with a single key inside.

"Lovely, Tony put a down payment on a house for us."

"A what?" I ask.

"A down payment on a house for us in New Jersey," JJ replies. "We can get out of our tiny flat—and with our new jobs—the payments will be easy. He put a lot of money down. Chance will have room to run."

"Why, JJ? Why do you think he might do that? And I love our tiny flat."

"He likes us, Lovely. I saved his life. He's a nice guy."

"No, JJ. I don't want to live in New Jersey. It's like Ohio and Brooklyn."

"What do you mean?"

"Gangsters and green, green grass."

"Lovely, it's the only thing I've ever really wanted in my whole life—besides you."

"Is it anywhere near your parents' house?"

"Of course not."

"Is it anywhere near Tony's house?"

"A few miles."

"But Lovely, there's a pool and room for Chance to run and I'll have a music room and it's just 30 minutes on Route 4 and across the George Washington Bridge to the city."

"I don't feel good about this."

Tears well up in his chocolate eyes.

"I need this house, Lovely."

"JJ, I love the city, we don't have a car, I'll never get to auditions. We work in the city."

"My parents gave us a car. Tony talked to them."

"What? That doesn't make sense."

"Lovely, they're not so horrible. My dad likes you."

"Your dad likes me because I can match him vodka shot for vodka shot, and I wear mini-skirts. The same two reasons your mother hates me."

"Well, we have a car. A white Pontiac Bonneville with a blue interior."

"That's the ugliest car ever made."

"Please, Lovely."

Needless to Say

In November of 1968, we move to Saddle Brook, New Jersey.

I am so strung out on who knows what that when the movers pull into the driveway with our furniture, I step fully clothed into the shallow end of the pool and walk on the bottom slowly to the deep end completely underwater. Chance panics and barks like crazy following me alongside the pool. I open my eyes underwater and see his face darting into and out of the pool. I hope to drown. Since no one but Chance notices me, I climb out and sit and shiver at the end of the diving board while my flower child turns into a suburban husband and second-rate gangster right before my eyes.

JJ makes nice with a neighbor. He accepts a campaign sign from him and they shake hands. JJ sticks the sign into our green, green grass. When the neighbor finally leaves, I slosh over and throw the sign into the trash.

After the first shock, I try to make the best of our new life. Tony gives us some time off work to play house and it's fun painting a bathroom black and a bedroom navy blue.

We drive into the city together in our white boat of a car. We park at the Warwick free, and JJ kisses me goodbye and walks the two blocks to his job at the Candy Store. At midnight I pick him up and he drives us home to New Jersey. He stays up most of the night writing, playing guitar and doing drugs. I drink until I get sick or fall asleep and develop a fondness again for orangish-reddish Seconals.

First I'm late for auditions and then when JJ doesn't even make an effort to go, I eventually stop auditioning, too. We quit the soap because it's too far to travel to the NBC studios in Queens and still get to our "job-jobs" on time. Besides we were little more than extras.

Tony likes me less and less as the days go by.

JJ works weekends, so basically I live alone with Chance in Saddle Brook, New Jersey.

Early one Saturday morning I drive out to Brooklyn to see my dad. He left early for the racetrack so I miss him, but my stepmother says I can take Vicki with me to Jersey. My half-sister is 12 now and adorable. We climb into the Bonneville and are laughing and talking when I hear something strange happen under the hood. I slow down to five miles per hour, lean over and open Vicki's door, and order her to roll out. She is horrified but does as I tell her. I stop the car about 50 feet from her. I rush back, grab her and we run as far from the car as we can get before it explodes. Totaled. Demolished. Destroyed. Vicki cries. Cars stop and people with fire extinguishers try to help us. The New Jersey Highway Patrol shows up and they give Vicki and me a ride to the house. Once I'm sure she's all right, I call a car service and send Vicki back to Brooklyn.

To me, losing the Bonneville is a good thing. We use the insurance payoff to buy a black Volkswagen bug, which is more my style. It never occurs to me to question the explosion.

One night when I drive over to pick up JJ after work as usual, the relief bartender tells me that JJ and Tony left earlier and the message for me is to go on home by myself. Instead I go to a bar opposite the Warwick Hotel and drink with some friends until four.

I am furious with JJ and I don't care that I'm too drunk to drive. I hit the Westside Highway at 50 and accelerate to 90. The Volkswagen won't go any faster than that. At first, I ignore the sirens thinking they're for someone else. Two cars, four cops, pull me over. I have an expired Ohio driver's license, I am drunk, and there are a couple of joints in the glove compartment. While one cop sits in the passenger seat, I lean over to say something to him and throw up in his lap. The other cops laugh, but he is not amused. They help me into a police car and drive me to the station.

Because I'm 23, look 12 and am nicely dressed for work, they are way too kind to me. At the station they offer to call my husband.

"He's not home and he doesn't care anyway. And I have the car. And I don't want a lawyer. Just lock me up, please."

I am pitiful. They put me in a comfortable padded room and bring me coffee, sandwiches and cookies. They talk and talk to me about the evils of driving while intoxicated, the evils of speeding.

At dawn, when I am completely sober, they give me two Excedrin and release me.

JJ is home when I get there, but doesn't believe me when I tell him that I spent the night at a police station. He accuses me of being with John Hartford's guitarist who is staying at the Warwick. Enraged, he drives away in our only form of transportation.

That night, JJ does not come home. It's my fault. I'm a bad wife. So I drink Remy Martin from the bottle, putting a few drops in a dish for Chance. When I am good and drunk, I gather all the knives in the house. I have no plan for the knives. Chance follows me into the bathroom and I turn on the water for a bath—hot water with lots of *Badedas* or Vitabath or whatever we call the bubbles *du jour.*

"Out, Chance."

While the water fills the tub, I shred the towels, bathmat, and hand towels. I use the longest serrated knife to bang up the salmon colored sink, tub and toilet. It is a wasted effort; just little nicks and ruined expensive stolen knives.

I light a citrus-scented candle and step into the foamy bath. I lean back and soak and cry, until I cannot stop sobbing. Then I slip underwater and hope to drown. Chance's pink tongue and big black nose poke through the water and he starts drinking the extremely hot bubbly water. I giggle and nearly choke.

This is night one without a call from JJ. Night two passes and I can't find him anywhere. On night three, I call the FBI, the local police, and all the local hospitals.

"Lady, we can't do anything unless you think your husband was abducted and taken across the state line, or that illegal drugs are involved," a woman at the FBI tells me.

"I think he was abducted and that drugs are a big part of it."

Within an hour three FBI guys are at the door. It's the middle of the night, so we have coffee in the kitchen while I tell them about JJ and Tony, the house, the stolen goods. I even give them a few 8x10 glossies of JJ for the search. I am convinced that Tony has done something to JJ, but I have no proof. After they leave, I curl up with Chance on the king-size bed in the gold room where JJ and I sleep, and cry until I can't cry anymore.

The phone rings me awake early the next morning.

"This is Tony. What the hell are you doing to me? Listen, you, get dressed and get into the city. I need a word with you."

"I'm not feeling well."

"Be here at three."

"I am not coming into the city until JJ gets back. Besides,

he came by and took the VW while I was sleeping."

"Listen, I don't know where your pretty boy is. I would tell you if I knew."

"You're a liar."

I do not go into the city. I really am too sick for that.

Three days later JJ comes home. A woman driving a white station wagon drops him off around three in the afternoon. He comes in, says nothing, takes off his clothes and sits naked on the bed, completely strung out. When he finally focuses on me, he says, "Listen to this, Lovely—it's by Tim Hardin—it's called *"The Lady Came from Baltimore."*

After listening long enough, I look at him and see him for the boy he really is.

"JJ, who was that woman who dropped you off?" And where's the car?"

"Just a friend, Lovely. It's over anyway. And your precious car is in the garage."

He puts his arms around me.

"I was so afraid for you, so worried," I tell him. "You were with someone else and you didn't even call to let me know you were all right. I didn't even know you brought the car back."

JJ gently pushes me away and strums his guitar. I run downstairs to the music room and go through his stuff and find at least 20 amphetamine bottles, some empty, some full. I run back upstairs, open the full bottles and throw all the pretty pills at him. He continues singing and strumming and doesn't look up at me.

"No more drugs, JJ."

"OK, Lovely." And his half-closed eyes open a little more, but he doesn't really see me. He has stars in his eyes like a cartoon character.

"Why don't you just take them all?"

"The Lady Came From Baltimore."

I can't stand it. Facing Tony would be better than this.

I put Chance in the Volkswagen and pull out onto Fairlawn Avenue. I get halfway to the George Washington Bridge before I realize that I told JJ to take all the pills. I turn around and drive back, but I'm too late. He has already swallowed most of the loose pills and is nearly comatose.

I try to remember all the things I've seen in movies about what to do if someone overdoses. I walk him around. I call an ambulance. I put a cold cloth on his face; he has a seizure. He is rubbery and heavy and I walk him around until I hear sirens. Chance barks the whole time.

Two paramedics. Three police officers. They take his body, tie it to a stretcher and push him into the ambulance. When I crawl in after him, the driver looks at me.

"Hey, isn't this the guy that came up missing a few days ago?" he asks.

"He came home."

They hook him up to oxygen and some kind of IV. He looks dead and he's wrapped like a mummy in a white sheet. I follow the ambulance to Hackensack Hospital in the Volkswagen.

The emergency room is chaotic. Interns and nurses pull a curtain around his bed and pump his stomach while a doctor asks me what he's taken. I give the doctor all the bottles I had gathered from the bedroom; all prescriptions made out to Tony. I managed to scrape Tony's name off the bottles before they asked for them.

JJ will recover, but he needs 24-hour observation and there is no one available tonight. I spend the night alone with him in a round room with glass observation walls. Throughout the long night, students and doctors and nurses stand above us commenting on his progress.

It turns out I have only one book with me in my bag— *Long Day's Journey Into Night* by Eugene O'Neill. The irony does not escape me.

JJ's ankles and wrists are tied loosely to the corners of his bed. His eyes open once in a while, but he doesn't seem to be able to focus on anything. About five hours into the night, JJ screams, "I am not an animal. I am not an animal."

I kiss his forehead and push his stringy wet hair back from his face. He smells of vomit and drugs and something else that might be fear. Or I might be smelling my own fear. What kind of person am I? I almost killed my husband. In the morning, JJ is almost himself again. He eats toast, scrambled eggs, drinks coffee and laughs with the nurses. They offer me breakfast, but I'm not hungry.

"How are we doing, JJ? You seemed a little depressed when you came in. What's that all about?" the doctor asks.

And I lose it.

"Get out of here, you moron. He tried to kill himself. Happy people don't do what he did."

JJ laughs.

"Lovely, if you ever leave me, I promise I really will kill myself."

He doesn't skip a beat and asks me if I called Tony.

"Not yet."

"He'll be worried."

I call Tony from a payphone out by the elevators—not from the room.

"Did you tell anyone where JJ got his pills?"

"Yes, I told everyone."

"That does not make me happy."

"JJ was dying."

I hang up on Tony knowing I will face him soon enough. Let him worry.

After a few days, JJ is completely recovered physically, but the doctors are worried about his mental state and want to keep him for further observation.

He spends a few weeks at Hackensack Hospital. I dread his homecoming and I miss him, too. I drink my way through the waiting time.

Eventually I have to face Tony. After work one night I go over to the Candy Store and wait for him in his office. He comes in, closes the door, sits and stares across his messy desk at me.

"How's our boy?"

"He'll be fine."

"Do you know how much trouble you've caused me?"

"I was scared."

"Do you know what it means for me—for me—to have the FBI here? Here in my office?"

"You should have told me where he was."

"He asked me not to."

"Tell me now."

"It was just some girl he met. I think she was from Baltimore."

"I went out to see him this morning. Thanks for taking the labels off the prescriptions. You had me going there for a while."

Drinking and planning my escape fill my days and nights. I know as long as JJ threatens suicide, I won't leave him.

I want him to come home. I don't want him to come home. I want him to die. I don't want him to die. I want to disappear.

Chance licks my face.

"Come on, Chance. Let's walk in the neighborhood for a change."

Chapter 24

Back to Normal

JJ is home. Hackensack Psychiatric releases him one sunny August morning. He looks as good as he feels.

"I feel wonderful, Lovely. What have you been up to?"

What have I been up to? Every day for months I have visited him at the hospital. I've worked extra hours at the Warwick to make the payments on the house I never wanted—and I've cried. I can't upset him with all that.

"I met Anne Baxter, Gig Young, James Taylor, and Cary Grant at the Warwick. Lots of people. Mostly Chance and I isolated. I've become more dog-like and Blue died."

"Lovely, who's Blue?"

"Our fish. That beautiful Siamese Warrior Fish."

JJ looks at me. He doesn't remember Blue.

"I buried him in the backyard, near the pool."

Seems we are both happy he's home. We unpack the mass accumulation of stuff he had with him in the hospital.

"You didn't meet anybody while I was in hospital, did you?" he asks as he looks at me. "I mean, go out with anybody? There isn't anyone you'd rather be married to than me, is there?"

I kiss him on the cheek and continue to unpack.

"I hope you don't mind," he says. "I've invited a friend from the hospital over this weekend. She's really a good person, Lovely. I think you two will get along great. She's got a beautiful voice."

My heart sinks. I am lost and more alone than ever. JJ puts his arms around me. He's more fragile than I am.

"Have anybody over that you want. I work weekends now, though, and am off Tuesdays and Wednesdays."

"Lovely, I meant what I said at the hospital. I never want you to leave me. And if you do, I really will kill myself."

"I love you. It will never be over until it's over for you. You know I would die if you killed yourself."

He hugs me until my ribs ache.

His visitor doesn't show up, so JJ calls the hospital. He starts to cry when he hangs up.

"She killed herself, Lovely. Not 15 minutes after I was released from the psych ward."

Divorce

We slip into our old lives effortlessly. JJ is back at the Candy Store. He and Tony focus on a new club they're opening at the corner of 57th and Second Avenue. Judy's. They talked Judy Garland into lending her name to the place. JJ's name will be on the lease. He's the only one who can get a liquor license. They see fortunes ahead.

And so it goes, until one day I get strep throat and peritonitis. It's so bad that I can't speak. I am actually bedridden as they said in the old days, and housebound. I can still drink, but only Harvey's Bristol Crème. It soothes my tender throat. Chance cuddles next to me in the king-size bed. It's all I can do to get up to feed him and open the door to let him out a few times a day. I have never been so sick in my life.

One night JJ doesn't come home. Around four a.m. the phone rings. I pick it up, even though I can't talk, because I'm sure something has happened to JJ. It's JJ and he's stoned.

"It's me, Lovely," he says. "I've met someone special. You can get that divorce you've been thinking about now. I'll sign anything you want."

I make a sound something like, "Ehk." And slam down the phone.

I am torn in so many directions. I want a divorce. I hate that I chose the kind of man who would call to tell me he's found someone he loves more than he loves me when I can't say a word. I wonder if it's a man or a woman.

First thing in the morning I call a lawyer, a friend of my dad's, Sanford. He arranges my trip to Mexico for a quickie divorce. I don't want to give JJ an opportunity to change his mind—or me time to realize how frightened I am. I can picture myself down on my knees again begging him not to leave me.

It's Monday. On Wednesday we have to sign papers in Sanford's office on John Street in the city. JJ has our Volkswagen, so he picks me up at noon. His girlfriend is with him. I get in the backseat.

"Lovely, this is Linda."

I can't talk because of the pain in my throat and in my

heart. But she and I both smile. It's not her fault. I keep that thought all the way to the city.

Linda waits in the car while we go up to Sanford's office and sign divorce papers. Uncontested. Incompatible. Irreconcilable. That's us.

And then they drive me back to Jersey. I think about how I never wanted to get married, never wanted a divorce, never wanted to drink. All the things that ruined my mother's life are now ruining mine. The thought is fleeting but penetrating.

JJ gets out of the car and kisses me goodbye.

"Lovely, you know I will always love you. Have a safe trip. Have a Margarita for me."

"Please take good care of Chance while I'm gone. Just a few days, okay?"

He gets back into the car and waves to me as they drive away.

He doesn't look so beautiful to me now.

Chance barks and I run into the house.

Mañana

The next day I am on a plane to Mexico. I keep picturing JJ, Linda and Chance having a great time at our house in Jersey. I drink too much during the flight and fall asleep. I dream that JJ is running toward me with the wind blowing through his beautiful hair. He looks like my father as he approaches me—when he turns and runs away, he looks like my mother.

I wake up as we hit the runway in El Paso. There's a middle-aged paunchy man at the baggage area holding a sign that says, "Divorce."

"Welcome, *señora*. I am your lawyer."

He takes my bags and I half listen while he tells me he's also my translator and he will drive me across the border to Mexico for the divorce—and a little shopping if I'd like. He takes me to dinner and I learn to drink tequila shots with lemon and salt while he explains the divorce procedure.

"Do you wish to spend the night with me, *señora*?"

"No way."

I bite my tongue to keep from adding anything else to my comment.

He smiles and agrees to pick me up at eight o'clock. sharp—*mañana*.

Divorce Eve

I have a night to spend alone and a bottle of tequila to drink. The sky is full of stars that lead me up into the rocks behind the motel where I consider drinking myself to death. I fantasize that bandits will find me and kill me like the tourist warning signs advertise. Or that a rattler will bite me. I need something far more dramatic than divorce. I lean against a gigantic rock while I drink from the bottle and take in the comforting, yet eerie sounds of owls and coyotes. It's cold. I'm cold. I want to feel the cold run through me. I don't know how to lose someone. I don't know how to love. I hate myself. I miss Chance and decide he won't even remember me when I get back. I pass out up among the huge rocks above El Paso.

In the morning I am hung over. I make my way down the steep rocks to the motel. After the hottest then coldest shower I can stand, I put on my new black jumpsuit. It's perfect for a divorce or a funeral or a gunfight.

Anacin helps, lots of coffee and dry toast take away my queasiness. The lawyer arrives right on time and drives me into Mexico and up to the courthouse. I am herded into a room with about 20 other people. The judge takes his place. He reads aloud to us, but in Spanish, and at one point he stops and looks through the crowd and points at me and asks in English, "You're an actress?"
I nod. He goes back to reading.

In less than 30 minutes I am a divorcée. I catch the next flight back to Jersey and pack. Linda has already moved in. Her things are all over the house.

I stick a note to JJ's guitar telling him that I have taken Chance with me. "And P.S. You and I are divorced." I leave him the house, the car, the stuff in the house, and I call a cab for Chance and me to get away from New Jersey as fast as we can.

The City

Luckily, my old friend Patty Pratt came through and invited me to stay at her place in the city for as long as I want.

She's on the road with "Fiddler on the Roof" and her apartment on 15th Street off Seventh Avenue is empty. Chance and I settle in.

My throat heals in a few days—my heart never.

Chapter 25

Left to My Own Vices

I come out of a blackout sitting in the entryway of Daytop Village, a drug treatment center just half a block from where I'm staying on 15th Street. Sitting next to me is Peter who introduces himself as a recovering heroin addict turned counselor. His voice is soft.

"Come on inside," he says. "You must be freezing dressed like that."

For some reason I listen to him and follow him inside to his office. I am not cold so I don't know what he means about—"dressed like that."

"What are you on?"

"On?"

"Taking. What are you taking?"

"Nothing."

"Look, I've been watching you walk up and down this block all morning. You didn't know where you were going."

"I'm not going anywhere. I live up the block."

There are a lot of people in a larger room watching television. Mostly men.

"Look, I'd like you to come with me over to St. Vincent's Hospital for a checkup?"

"No."

Somehow he convinces me that it's a good idea to see someone, that something is wrong with me. He talks all the way up 15th Street to Seventh Avenue and all the way down to 13th Street to the hospital. We go inside and he whispers something to the admissions woman who directs us to the back.

They take my blood, my blood pressure, my temperature.

"She's dehydrated, probably anemic," he tells a nurse.

Peter stays with me while they hook up the IV.

"Do you eat?"

"Of course I eat."

Now that I am fully out of the blackout and realize what I've gotten myself into, I am not happy at all. Not angry. Just sad. Just tired. Peter's voice sounds far away.

"We work with a couple of good psychiatrists here. Would you talk to mine if he's in?" he asks.

"Sure. Why not? I like psychiatrists." Even now I am the people-pleaser. I make myself sick.

While he is gone, the nurse continues the exam and asks questions.

"Do you get a lot of headaches? How much water do you drink? Alcohol? Do you take any drugs?"

"I'm just tired. Hung over."

"What drugs have you taken today?"

"None, really. Just Excedrin or Anacin. I smoked some grass last night; maybe it was hash. I don't remember."

"Tell me what you do remember."

"I was at the Haymarket—a restaurant. The chef, a friend of mine, waved to me and I went into the kitchen. He offered me his hashish pipe. I smoked and smoked with him. When I went back out into the restaurant, everything was gone."

"What do you mean everything?"

"People, tables, the bar, sounds, everything. Gone."

The nurse writes something on her chart and leaves.

I lie in the bed staring at a poster that shows the inside of a mouth, the tongue, and all its parts, in full grotesque color. The psychiatrist and Peter come in and stand on either side of my bed.

"This is Steve, Dr. Adler."

"Hello, Dr. Adler," I mumble.

"Peter, you can go now. Your friend and I will talk alone."

I thank Peter for I know not what and he is gone.

"Do you know the meaning of the word paranoia?" are the first words out of the doctor's mouth.

I stare at him. I hate him.

"Do you think I'm an idiot? Of course I know the meaning of the word paranoia."

"I want you to come to my office tomorrow at noon. Can you do that?"

"I can. But I won't."

"Then get this prescription filled."

"What is it?"

"Mood stabilizer—Elavil. And don't drink with it."

The doctor leaves and I cry quietly until snot runs down my face and the nurse returns to take the IV out of my arm. I thank her for her kindness and leave the first chance I get.

It's cold outside.

I can't wait to get home. But when I get there I am alone. I look around and am happy that my apartment is clean. Nothing is out of place except me.

Lying on my back on the twin bed, staring at cracks in the off-white ceiling, I listen to car alarms, fire engine sirens, children yelling, men shouting in Spanish. I hear a dog bark in the apartment next door. I miss Chance. He lives upstate in the country with JJ now. He can finally be a dog.

Then across my narrow gray bedroom I see something move. It's a dust ball so I go over to pick it up. It runs under my dresser. It's not dust; it's a mouse. I can call the super. I can move, but where? I'm living on unemployment in Patty's apartment, which we now share semi-permanently. It's convenient for both of us. She's always on the road.

I grab a two-week old copy of the *Village Voice* from my magazine basket and read through the pet section.

That's what I need. I call. They're still available. The next thing I know, I'm in some stranger's apartment on 14th Street and I've picked out two Siamese kittens from the same litter, and I am back home with them, their food, litter box, bowls, toys, collars. They are six weeks old and I put them in my bedroom thinking they'll catch mice.

But I fall in love with Cain and Abel anyway even though they are useless in the mouse department. They will rule my life now. I am not alone. I thought I liked being alone. And in a way I do, but I need something alive around me. I don't have enough life myself.

It's only noon. I have a few hours before work, so I take a nap with the kittens. They lie on my head and calm me, small as they are. I sleep until the alarm shatters the silence at 2:30 p.m.

I shower and dress and walk over to Sixth Avenue to catch the uptown bus. I can't believe I'm still working at the Warwick. I smile to myself—the mafia connection paid off after all. They like my work well enough to take me back every time I finish an acting job. The manager arranges for all my actor friends to work at other hotels in the Loew's chain. I love helping my friends and four to midnight is good for all of us. Patty and her best friend from the Oklahoma mafia—Rick

Northcutt—and I all end up working at Loew's hotels. Usually we meet afterward at the Haymarket to drink and whine about the famous and not-so-famous guests.

Chapter 26

Hotel

Always on time, I'm at my post at the front desk at exactly four o'clock. Thursdays are usually quiet, so I work the desk alone and handle room reservations and guest complaints, as well.

Cary Grant is on the Board of Fabergé so he lives in the Fabergé suite at the Warwick, and I look forward to his arrival every evening that he's in town. Always charming. Soon I see him coming through the revolving door into the lobby. He has his little girl perched on his shoulders and she is giggling. They are magnificent. I smile at him and reach for his mail in the box behind me. I trip over something and fall flat out behind the desk. Cary Grant puts his daughter down on the front desk and leans across to help me up.

"You all right?" he asks.

I pop up. Embarrassed, of course. I crack heads with him. We both laugh and as he takes his mail and walks away with his daughter, I cry. This crying thing is making me crazy.

I eat dinner in the dining room—alone on Thursdays. The other days of the week another staff member—Maureen or Angelo or Gerry—will join me. These are my perks: good food and the quiet of an empty dining room.

Francesco, a jockey-sized busboy from El Salvador, excitedly points out Frank Sinatra at another table across the room.

"Mr. Sinatra thought you was Mia Farrow and was ready to leave. I tell him, 'No, Mr. Sinatra, it's the room clerk.' He asks if you would face the other direction while you eat."

"No, Francesco, I won't."

"OK. OK."

He goes into the kitchen.

I finish my meal quickly and get back to the desk. My dinner hour ruined.

My favorite guest—Gig Young, an underrated actor who is finally nominated for an Academy Award for *They Shoot Horses, Don't They?*— waits at the front desk.

He spends half my shift with me, leaning on the front desk. We share a bottle of champagne while he tells stories of his life. It's fascinating to me that he took his name from the first character he ever played. He liked seeing it on the screen, Gig Young played by Gig Young.

"My television isn't working so well and I'm on Johnny's show tonight. Think you can get somebody up to my room to fix it?"

"There's no engineer on duty, but you can watch it in the office on our television if you want. Or the bar."

"Too many people in the bar. Will anyone be watching your television?"

"Just me now that I know you're going to be on."

"I'll watch with you."

Johnny Carson destroys Gig Young the way only he can. He implies that Gig is gay and makes gay jokes all night. Part way through the show, Gig says goodnight and goes up to his room. He's devastated and not interested in watching the rest of his segment.

At midnight, the doorman hails a cab for me. I'm a little drunk but not nearly drunk enough.

Back home, I cuddle with Cain and Abel and finish a bottle of Remy Martin. Cain and Abel lie on my chest as I drink from the bottle. I don't want to disturb them. Besides, it's too much trouble to get up and get the crystal brandy snifter I love so much.

I think about calling my mother to tell her and Darryl about the kittens and Frank Sinatra, but it's too late. They'll be asleep by now. I miss them tonight. I know my mother's okay because Leonard is with her. I know she doesn't love the suburban life she always dreamed of, but I am so happy that she's sober and at least starting to have a life.

Fool Moon Maybe

Another night at the front desk. Tonight is chaos. Too many late check-ins. Too many celebrities.

A guy I met when he stayed at the hotel—whose name I can never remember—has a friend of his in Room 810. I avoid him as much as I can—partly because he's good looking in a ghoulish way and partly because he's been a guest at the hotel for a week, so I assume he has plenty of money. I am always fearful that rich people might think I want something from them. What a strange mood I'm in.

Whenever Howie—that's the guest's name—sees me at

work, he saunters over to talk about our mutual friend. And I remember his name now, it's Mitch something or other. All I know about this Howie is that when he was cold one night I gave him a beige V-neck cashmere sweater that belonged to JJ and that had somehow ended up among my sweaters when I left in such a hurry. It was a birthday gift to JJ from me, so when Howie didn't return it, I didn't ask for it back.

A man at the desk crashes into my thoughts. For the life of me, tonight I can't remember his name, either. He hates filling out the registration card because he stars in the television show *Marcus Welby* opposite Robert Young and I'm the desk clerk and I should know he's *somebody*.

Howard Cosell shows up next with his entourage and I misspell his name on his registration card. He grabs the card out of my hand and indignantly finishes filling it out all by himself. Howard Cosell with a K or a C is sufficiently annoying to ruin my mood for the night.

I recognize Wayne Newton, but I can't stand the way he treats his beautiful Asian wife, who is less than half his size. So I'm not too pleasant to him. She acts like an employee, ready to be fired at the first wrong step.

Then Anne Baxter, one of my all-time favorite actresses (mainly because of her role in *All About Eve*), who is modest, beautiful and charming, shows up and I register for her and wave her on because I know she cannot wait to get away from the crowd at the front desk and into the darkness of the bar.

And Johnny Mathis' exotic-looking brother signs in for both of them without my having to ask. He hands me four tickets to a Mathis concert. There is so much activity I am barely able to mouth the words "thank you" as he walks away with the bellman.

Around 11 o'clock, activity slows to a stop and I can take a short break, which means I sit on a stool in an out of the way corner but still behind the front desk. What is happening tonight? It's not even a holiday.

The desk phone rings through to me. It's that guy Mitch from Room 810. His voice is a whisper on the other end.

"Don't say anything," he says. "Just listen. I'm in jail. This is my one phone call. I need a favor. You can save my life. Go to my room. Under the mattress is a plastic bag. Just get the bag and save it for me."

"What's in the bag?"

"Will you please just get it out of my room and save it for me? I'll make it worth it to you."

He hangs up. I ask a bellman to watch the desk.

"I have to check one of the rooms."

I have a master key and I check rooms occasionally when the assistant manager isn't around, so it's no problem for me to get into 810. The room is messy, clothes thrown around. Slobs like Mitch irritate me; like people who throw their trash on the floor at a movie because that's what people do. But under the mattress, as promised, is a large, white garbage bag. Inside are hundreds and hundreds of loose pills in all the colors of the rainbow—and more. I pick out a few scoops of Seconals because I still like that orangish-reddish color—not to mention the way they knock me out. For a split second, I consider keeping them all, but I change my mind and spend the next few minutes flushing the rest of the pills down the toilet. There are so many that I flush several times to make sure they're all gone. I hope they don't clog up the plumbing. It's an old hotel.

When I get back to the front desk, two detectives are waiting for me. I look at their badges and take a deep breath. One asks for the key to 810. I give the master key to the bellman and he takes the detectives to the waiting elevator.

The police search and find nothing, but after they leave I go upstairs to see what they've done only to find they sealed off the room with bright yellow warning tape so I can't go back in.

It's just about midnight when I get a call from the drug dealer's lawyer. Midway through the call, I tell him.

"I flushed it all down the toilet before the police got here."

He hangs up on me.

I wish I'd never heard of Howie or Mitch or whatever they call themselves.

Back at my apartment, the Seconals look really pretty in the crystal brandy snifter on my dresser. The rest of my room is dull, gray, and funereal. I've got to get out of here. Cain and Abel are asleep. They look peaceful and I wish I were a cat.

Friday and Saturday are my days off this week, but I decide not to go back to the Warwick for a few days. I am tired of the drama. And I'm a little afraid of what Mitch the drug dealer and his mighty lawyer will do to me. I've heard nothing from them since that night. Howie might remember where I live because he was here once, but Mitch doesn't know.

Locked In, Lucked Out

Of course, I can't quit my job-job until I find another one or get an acting job, so I am stuck working at the hotel. One warm midnight after working seven days in a row, instead of going straight home after work, I walk over to Jimmy Ryan's, a jazz club on 52nd Street. It's only two blocks down and one over and I feel comfortable there even when I'm by myself, partly because my dad introduced me to the musicians years ago and told them to keep an eye on me and partly because it's a hangout for the people who work at the Warwick.

The place is packed, just coming to life. The regular bartender sees me and points to a kind of half booth in the corner near the quartet and not far from the end of the bar. I mouth "thank you." He sends over a scotch on the rocks.

The Eddie Clocke Jr. Quartet is playing. Eddie is a drummer's drummer. I think he or another musician in the group and my dad might have been roommates in Miami in the 1940s, when my dad was going through his saxophone days. Dad introduced me to Eddie just once.

As soon as I finish my drink another one appears and the bartender keeps them coming. I relax and lean back to listen to the music. I'm so tired and I can drink with my eyes closed.

I listen while one of the other bartenders, probably an out-of-work actor, insults Nichol Williamson, a successful and abusive drunken English actor sitting at the bar. He keeps calling him Mr. Nicholson instead of Williamson. "Yes, Mr. Nicholson. Of course, Mr. Nicholson, I know who you are. Mr. Nicholson."

Time Flies

The next time I open my eyes, I am in a strange place and it must be hours later because morning light is filtering through Venetian blinds. The photo on the wall across from me has an inscription that reads: to Eddie, the greatest drummer in the world. I am in Eddie Clocke's bedroom. In Eddie Clocke's bed. I lie there for a while staring at the closed door. Someone is lying next to me. A heavy breather. I look down at myself. I have all my clothes on: my navy blue Warwick desk clerk uniform of sorts, pants, a white blouse, a navy blue jacket. I even have my shoes on. I see my brown Coach bag on the floor. Oh, god, what have I done this time?

I lie quietly and listen to the noises outside the room. There must be 50 people out there and the music and voices are so loud.

Slowly I lift my left arm and check my watch. Five on the nose. I twist around onto my right side. Thank you, god. It's Eddie. He is lying on his back sound asleep. Naked. And he has an erection. I stare at him. His skin is magnificent against the pale blue sheet. His penis is almost the color of eggplant.

I turn back around, sit up and the room spins. I have to get out of here. I tiptoe to the bathroom and pee without flushing. Please don't let Eddie wake up.

When I open the door, I am standing in the center of the living room and there's a party going on. I turn back to look at Eddie. He is beautiful. When I face the living room again, about 20 people are staring at me. I am the only white person there.

A motherly woman rescues me and walks me to the front door. She opens the police lock and three more.

Someone yells, "Goodbye, Sleeping Beauty."

Someone else shouts, "More like Snow White."

The woman smiles and puts her arm around me.

"You give Shiekie my regards. Tell him Joanne asked about him. You look just like your father."

Outside the door I hear all the locks on Eddie Clocke's door as Joanne bolts them.

I'm afraid of heights and I don't see an elevator, just a winding staircase down what looks like five flights. I make it to the bottom, one step at a time. To the lobby. Outside. I have no idea where I am. I search through my pockets and bag and find two pennies and a nickel. The streets are deathly quiet for New York. There are no taxis to wave down. I walk, hoping I'm heading downtown. I have the worst sense of direction. I finally find Broadway and numbered streets again. I'm in Harlem. If I didn't have such a headache, I'd be all right.

At the top of the steps leading down to the subway station, there is an old man sitting on a wooden crate. He talks to his dog and laughs.

I start to cry.

The old man turns to me.

"What the fuck are you looking at? What are you, lost?"

"I need money for the subway. Can you help me, please?"

He considers me for a long time, reaches in his pocket, takes out a handful of change, goes through it and finds a subway token.

"Go home."

"Thank you."

"Go home."

The bright fluorescent lights on the "A" train burn my eyes and the swaying car makes me nauseous. I vomit and cover the mess with a page from a newspaper that is wadded up on the seat next to me.

I look around to see if anyone notices. These people are probably going to work. They are not interested in my vomit or me. I hate myself. I am too white. Too stupid. My mouth is too dry. I swear I will never drink like that again—when I am already so tired.

I don't want to look directly at anyone, so I stare at their shoes. My shoes. The train rattles on. At every stop more people get on. They avoid me and my stench as best they can.

A woman with red hair gets on at 125th Street and I think of my mother. I never understood why she promised me things a hundred times a week and forgot what she promised a hundred times a week. She promised amusement parks, duck feeding, zoos and Paris to buy toys. The next day she'd remember nothing. I didn't know then that I was growing up in my mother's blackouts. That we would never say to each other "remember when?" She does not remember my childhood. All my bad memories are mine. And now I'm making my own.

I thought blackouts were normal after living in hers for so long. Right now I feel like they're anything but normal. I have to stop drinking so much. I wonder if you die during a blackout, or get killed on a subway, if you're really dead.

I'm 25, look 15 and feel 90.

No wonder my mother drank so much. This life thing is as hard as Eddie Clocke's dick.

Chapter 27

The Second Time Around

Patty's on the road again. This time my buddy from Oklahoma is in another production of *Fiddler on the Roof.* I have the apartment to myself.

All my old friends rally round, but I am beyond human help. I am disappointed, depressed, defeated, and I remember I never wanted to get married, never wanted to drink, never wanted to feel this kind of pain.

My brother Darryl is still a little bit annoyed with me for divorcing JJ. I can't tell him the whole story because it hurts too much. Mother puts her two cents in.

"I'm surprised he stayed with you as long as he did."

My dad says, "I could have told you that guy was a jerk. Good looking, but not as good looking as I am."

Finally I get a call that they're taking *Play It Again, Sam* out on the road again. It's a small role, but I take it anyway. I have a week to get my life in order.

Seeing Mother

I take the shuttle in from the Cleveland Airport to Fairlawn. Mother and Darryl pick Cain, Abel and me up in front of the Hilton. Darryl is sixteen and gorgeous. Mother looks fabulous. She's working at Lerner's at Summit Mall.

"You'll never guess who I have lunch with every day. Dottie."

I smile. I wouldn't have guessed. Dottie helped Mother get sober. They've been friends a long time now.

"Once a week we exchange gifts. She works at another shop in the mall."

I am happy for my mother. She has a friend. She has a life.

At dinner Leonard shows me a copy of "The Wingfoot," Goodyear's employee newsletter. He reads aloud, "Leonard Zito's daughter gets role in *Play It Again, Sam.*" He adds, "Photo and all. I hope you don't mind I said daughter, not stepdaughter."

I get up from the table and give him a big hug. Mother

laughs. Darryl smiles.

In the morning after Leonard leaves for work and Darryl goes to school, I wander around the house while Mother showers and gets ready. The first thing I notice is that she replaced the wedding photograph of JJ and me with an 8x10 of JJ alone. She adored him.

She is slow to start, but otherwise we have a good time together. I notice she takes a little yellow pill from time to time throughout the day. At The Egg and I where we go for lunch she tells me she got a promotion at Lerner's, that she's made more sales than all the other girls put together. And then she takes another one of those yellow pills.

"For my nerves."

Hit the Road

I fly directly from Cleveland to somewhere in the southwest where I join my friend Carole Anne Allen in yet another dinner theatre production.

I was in a daze of depression, drugs and drinking when I got this job, but after a sobering week in Akron and sober rehearsal week, I'm doing pretty well. I share a townhouse with Carole who is traveling with her white cat named Critter. I miss Cain and Abel. I left them in Ohio with Mother and Leonard and Darryl. It never occurred to me to bring them on the road. Next time.

Carole almost immediately gets involved with an actor in the show, so Critter and I become roommates. I drink and smoke grass and watch the rather crazy Critter run into the bare white wall like it's a snowstorm.

As usual, I enjoy doing the show, but avoid opening night celebrations, all celebrations, by hiding in my dressing room until the noise dies down. Onstage I am fine—not depressed, not sick, almost happy. Offstage I am the same lost soul I always am.

From Dallas we take the show to Fort Worth and then on to Scottsdale, Arizona. I love Arizona because I can take long walks in the Arizona sun and wear out one pair of moccasins at a time.

I now black out every time I drink. I learn that not everyone blacks out and that not everyone wants to die every day.

A Year and a Road

After a year on the road, one of the actors leaves the show

and his replacement is a tall, blonde leading man named Ted. I meet him for the first time in the station wagon on the way to the theatre. I have on a red tank top and faded blue jeans and the worn-out moccasins. My bleached blonde hair is in hot rollers.

He laughs out loud, right in my face, when we are introduced.

After the show I wait alone in my dressing room while the rest of the cast mingles with the audience. Ted finds me. He has a scotch on the rocks for each of us.

"You looked so absolutely absurd when I first laid eyes on you. I had no idea who you were when I saw you onstage." I drink my scotch and he pours more. He drinks J&B; I like Johnny Walker Black.

I am falling in love again.

On the way home that first night, Ted is so drunk he cannot speak; and can barely stand—let alone walk. Now everyone else in the cast is worried about him and afraid he'll cause trouble and get us all thrown out of our fancy townhouses.

Carole leans over and whispers.

"Take him home with you."

The guys half-carry him into my townhouse. He passes out on my bed. I try to take off his denim jacket, but he's like a corpse. A gorgeous cowboy corpse.

When I wake up in the morning the sheet is cold and damp. Ted opens his bloodshot blue eyes.

"Damn, not again." He grins. "I got a bladder the size of a pea."

He gets up, kisses me on my forehead, dresses and leaves.

Big City Ted

At the end of the run, Ted goes back to New York with me where we live together off and on in the tiny apartment he rents on Restaurant Row—one room facing 46th Street and its neon signs.

When I finally get Cain and Abel back from Ohio, I move them in with Ted, too. They sleep with us. I cuddle with them after Ted passes out.

Ted doesn't have a job yet. He's on unemployment until he finds something. I am collecting unemployment, too.

All we have in his apartment are a bed and a chair and a table. A friend of mine loans him a radio. I am not drinking as much as I was because I'm worried about Ted all the time.

He is not home this rainy night in the early 1970s. I feed the cats and stay awake as long as I can. I have to choose a monologue for an audition the next day. Not drinking makes me sleepy.

Around four a.m., the phone rings me awake. A man's voice.

"Do you know a tall, good-looking dude, calls himself Ted?"

"Who is this?"

"He's lying in a pool of his own blood right in the street next to this phone."

"Where are you?"

"Eighth Avenue and 48th Street. Southwest corner."

Click.

I throw on my clothes and some kind of shoes and run out of the building and into the street to find a cab. There's one stopped outside Broadway Joe's.

Maybe I should walk. No, I don't know who this guy is.

At 48th Street, I see Ted sitting on the curb smoking a cigarette.

"Driver, please stop. And please wait for me."

I jump out of the cab.

"I'm picking up a friend. Please wait."

"Darlin', what are you doing here?"

Ted lifts his shirt.

"Look at this. Some fool stuck me with a knife."

Thank god, it's just a tiny cut. Some dried blood. There's no one else anywhere near the payphone.

"Darlin', they took my wallet and everything."

"Everything?"

"My keys, my I.D. and stuff."

"Can you stand up?"

He holds onto a trashcan and pulls himself all the way up.

"Ted, get in the cab."

"Well, sure, honey."

"Please take us to 46th and Eighth," I tell the cabbie.

Ted is so drunk he's goofy.

"I met some real nice guys, tonight. Actors. I've got a card.

One of them was from Tulsa."

He searches through his empty pockets; turns them inside out like a little kid.

We reach our destination. I pay the driver and give him a huge tip. Embarrassment and gratitude. Then I coax Ted up the stairs all the while thinking about how I used to do this with my mother. It was easier with her. She wasn't the size of a racehorse. The door is wide open. Cain and Abel. I find them huddled together under the bed.

"My radio's gone."

Ted stumbles around.

"My money."

And he opens a cupboard door.

"My money. My answering machine."

They used our new magenta pima cotton pillowcases to carry their meager haul.

"Ted, we have to get the locks changed."

"Why? You don't think the guys from tonight did it? They were actors."

"They have your keys."

We prop a chair up against the door and go to sleep.

The cats stay under the bed all night. Just as well. Ted pees all over everything during the night.

When I wake and think about the night before, I am so glad he's alive and remembered my name so that guy could call me or I would have been asleep when they came for the borrowed radio.

Ted needs to stop drinking. Know it all me. This morning it's easy to talk him into calling AA. We talk about leaving the city, moving to Brighton Beach to be near the ocean while he sobers up. He calls the AA hotline. Goes to a meeting.

He cleans up and within 90 days finds a sober girlfriend and disappears with her into looming stardom. He gets a TV series that runs for a long time. I cannot watch his show. He is a good actor though and deserves his celebrity. I tell myself this as I sit alone in the Brighton Beach apartment that we had talked about sharing.

A year or two later I run into Ted outside the Carnegie Tavern. He invites me to have coffee with him and he does his AA amends. I smile and apologize, too, and wish him well. He is beautiful and on his way home to Los Angeles where his wife raises German Shepherds while he does his TV series. I tell him how well I am doing, too, and how happy I am. And he believes me.

I see Ted just two more times in my life—when I move to Los Angeles. Once he is crossing Sunset at Doheny and I am stopped at a light in my battered blue Volvo. *"Run him over,"* says a voice in my head. I watch until he's safely on the other side of Sunset before I drive on.

The second time is at the Emmy Awards in 1982 when Tom, my second husband, wins a sound editing award for *Inside the Third Reich*, and Ted presents the Emmy to him. All my friends watching at home get a chuckle out of that charming coincidence.

Chapter 28

Moved to Tears

I keep drinking—not realizing I have a serious problem, too. I unwittingly planned my move to Brooklyn very well. I'm near my dad and the ocean and I have all the time in the world to be alone. To think. It's winter and an apartment across from the ocean is cheap this time of year. Rents aren't usually that low, but after all, I'm Shiekie's daughter, Betty's stepdaughter. Besides it's a dark and gloomy apartment facing the alleyway that no one else wants. They don't even want it in the summer. It's been vacant for five years and it has an empty unwanted feeling.

I consciously isolate now. Cain and Abel are my only companions. My dad rarely visits me, nor does anyone else in the family although they are all only a block and a half away. When I venture out, I take the long way to the El so as not to pass the building where my aunts, uncles, cousins and grandfather live.

Once a week I take the D train into the city and see yet another psychiatrist. I want to be someone else. I'm sick of who I am. But this doctor is definitely not the one who is going to help me. He keeps me well supplied with pills: antidepressants, anti-psychotics, anti-seizures, and tranquilizers. They all go nicely with the Seconals and expensive white wine I drink every night. The vomit isn't as ugly as it is with red. I much prefer red, but this is a choice I have to make.

Sometimes I walk on the Boardwalk to Coney Island and think about the fun I had there when I was a kid, about all the freaks. About how I am a freak. I usually walk home in the cold wet sand at the water's edge. I like the feeling of my feet being sucked into the sand. Occasionally I walk in the other direction from Coney Island to Manhattan Beach where the rich people live.

Depression comes in waves. I hate myself when I think in such trite terms. No creativity left. I realize how dull I am. I stare at the horizon and see my head aglow and watch my smiling face set like the bright orange sun.

November. I write my age in the sand with a piece of

driftwood. Then I sit there bonding with seagulls. I love seagulls. They don't seem so afraid of me anymore. I think about how Barbara Hershey changed her name to Seagull when a gull died during the filming of Evan Hunter's "Last Summer." She beat me out for the lead role in that film. Both of us were unknowns. Then.

I wear gray all the time. It's my costume for this pitiful period of my life. I obsess about my failed marriage to JJ, failed career as an actress, failed relationship with Ted. I think about my childhood and feel guilty for the thoughts. I miss my mother and Darryl and Leonard and wonder if they ever think about me.

I am hiding out in my own witness protection program. My *witless* protection program. I laugh out loud at the pun and frighten the seagulls away. The lowest form of humor, someone said, is a pun.

No job. Little money. Cain, Abel and a brand new GE apartment-size refrigerator. I collect shells and rocks and run with stray dogs on the beach. No TV, no connection to the world except a phone that I do not answer. And now it never rings.

I try to stop drinking by limiting myself to two glasses of wine a day, but then thinking takes its place. I might as well be dead.

My dad surprises me one morning when he stops by with a friend.

"Geez. This place would depress me. And get rid of these cats, they're making me nuts. What do you want with an animal whose only claim to fame is it can shit in a box?"

Soon I am completely numb, so I call a psychiatric hotline and get the number of another psychiatrist. I carry the number with me on my walks. I sleep with it. I sleep a lot. I promise myself I will call the first time I feel good enough to talk. The holidays are coming and I try to forget that.

Late in December my phone rings. I stare at it. It rings every day for a week. I might have to answer it—or take it off the hook—if it doesn't stop ringing soon.

Chapter 29

Chuck, the First Time

Months at the beach wasted and now it's almost spring. Time to put the phone back on the hook. That damnable, ringing phone. I am almost out of the money I saved doing my last play and being a transcriber at night in the English Unit at the UN during the General Assembly. I pay bills because I have to, drink cheaper wine and eat less. I have a cupboard full of Friskies and Kal-Kan. And with all the sand across the street, I still have to buy kitty litter in five pound bags because the 10-pounders are too heavy to carry the three blocks from the grocery to my apartment.

For variety and out of habit, I travel to the city on the D train once a week to see that supplier of useless pharmaceuticals. I take the pills. I sleep. I don't cry as much I used to. Now my goal is to become invisible.

One afternoon on my return from the beach, the now-bearded and very handsome Chuck Pfahl is standing outside my building waiting for me. It is a cruelly beautiful day. He wears a blue velvet jacket, or maybe it is green. And jeans.

"How did you find me?" I ask.

"Your father. But it wasn't easy. Don't you ever answer your phone?"

"No. Never."

"Aren't you going to invite me in?"

I don't want him to see the way I live.

"Chuck, it's beautiful out. Why don't we walk to Coney Island? It's so close."

We walk in silence breathing in the clean sea air. Chuck is Chick and Dottie's son. They were my mother's sponsors in AA all those years ago. We didn't meet until I married John. I like Chuck. I wonder if he knows our mothers are still best friends. I know that after many years of marriage, his dad left his mother for a younger, kinder, non-alcoholic un-addicted woman. My mother told me Dottie took it hard and went back to drinking and drugging. That if she didn't stop soon, she'd die. In the mid-1960s, when Chuck moved to New York, he stayed with JJ and me in our eastside walkup apartment. When he married Evie, she joined him in New York, and JJ helped them get an really small apartment next to the Candy Store on 56th Street. He got Chuck a job at the Candy Store, too. Evie was pregnant then and the most beautiful girl becoming a woman I had ever seen.

"How's Evie?"

Chuck looks at his watch. I look, too. It has a wide brown leather band with the watch centered.

"Divorced."

"Are you still living in that great apartment on Eastern Parkway?"

"No, I'm in a loft in the city—Hell's Kitchen. It's a bare space, but I'm working on it, little by little."

We walk on in quiet comfort until we reach Coney Island.

"Hungry?" he asks.

"No."

"I am."

"Nathan's is just around the corner. Greatest hotdogs in the world. French fries to die for. At least they used to be good when I was a kid and spent summers out here."

Nathan's has not changed one iota. Delicious hotdogs and French fries in cone-shaped cups. I order an orange drink, hot dog and fries.

"Thought you weren't hungry?" Chuck says.

We go into the little dining room in the alley beside Nathan's. It hasn't changed either. My memory shoots me back to Jo-Jo the Dog Faced Boy and the others who were kind to me when I was little. I wish they were here now, but I'm glad I'm not a child anymore.

When we get back to my apartment, I feel I have to invite Chuck in. He's a talented artist with incredibly good taste, so I'm afraid the way I live will shock him. I was right to be concerned about his opinion. He is appalled at the way I am living. He doesn't say much about it, but I can see the pity in his crystal-clear blue eyes.

"Do you have a bathroom?"

"Through the bedroom."

I wash the dirty coffee mugs in the sink while he's gone and scoop poop from the litter box. Chuck returns smiling.

"That's a cave, not a bedroom."

So I smile, too. It is a cave. I wonder what he thinks about my twin beds lined up head to foot on one side of the long room.

"Why don't you put your beds together? You'd have a heck of a lot more space, and you'd be more comfortable."

"I like the small bed. One small bed. Cain and Abel sleep on the other one when they get tired of me rolling over on them."

I see how dark the living room is now, too, with the bare light bulb hanging from the ceiling in the middle of the room.

"Let's go get some dessert or something."

We climb into his old blue Chevrolet, the one he drove from Ohio to New York years ago. I direct him to Sheepshead Bay and we go to Lundy's, the greatest seafood restaurant on the east coast.

"Sorry you didn't think of this place earlier. What kind of desserts do they have?"

"Key Lime Pie."

"Sold."

We lighten up again as we drink our coffee and share three pieces of the pie.

"Don't you miss the city?"

I shake my head.

"What happened with acting?"

I hunch my shoulders up and then let them drop down again.

"I have 5,000 square feet of loft space. You can come and stay with me if you want."

"What about Cain and Abel?"

"Them, too, of course. Think about it."

And then he's gone.

Afterward, I think about his invitation. This wasn't spur of the moment. It must have been Chuck calling all winter. Chuck has come to save my life.

After a few more visits from Chuck, bearing gifts—flowers, food for the refrigerator, and a light fixture to cover up the bare bulb—and an afternoon or two of wine and love in the cave, I move to the loft and leave the ocean to the seagulls. The ocean fed my depression and I'm full now.

Chapter 30

Lofty Ideals

The move is a blur.

Chuck and a couple of his friends rent a U-Haul truck and take my belongings to the loft on 45th Street—a fifth-floor walkup in an ancient factory building. Two floors of the building still operate as businesses. The other floors are occupied by artists and musicians. I like Hell's Kitchen. I always have. It's seedy, diverse and used condoms line the streets like deflated remnants of some kind of weird parade.

His loft is on the top floor and it is as light as my cave was dark. I have always loved Chuck's work, but actually being in his studio is a religious experience. His work is magnificent. The smell of oil paint and turpentine are magical. It's all studio space with the living space carved into it. It is heaven and everything in it is beautiful.

Chuck cleaned the raw space and added a bathroom and a makeshift kitchen. My white GE apartment-sized refrigerator looks ridiculously out of place in his world. But I think I can be happy here and I know I can learn a lot about art and even more about how to live from Chuck.

Unfortunately, Cain and Abel immediately start torturing Persia, Chuck's gray Persian cat, and she is forced to make the top of the refrigerator her home.

While I wander around the loft, I think back to when I first met Chuck. His parents, Chick and Dottie, my mother's sponsors in AA, brought him to our wedding reception. He spent a lot of time with us that weekend because he and JJ hit it off and I liked him, too. I wished then that we'd met earlier and been friends during the dark days in Akron. He reminded me that I had come to his house once with my mother to meet him and he hid in the basement because he was too shy to come upstairs to meet me. We've been friends ever since my first wedding reception. I still have a small photo JJ took the day after our wedding of my dad, Chuck and me.

Chuck helps me re-enter New York life and face my social phobia now that he has conquered his to some extent. He has so many friends, mainly artists, who live in the other lofts in our building and another smaller building in the back. I like them all. They seem to like me, too.

Kees, Jason, Rose and Skee are pursuing their artistic dreams and living in the New York art world of the 70s.

Chuck's self-contained apartment within the huge loft is a cocoon where I feel safe. His personality is strong and his life force mammoth enough to encompass me and pull me along.

In our miles of icy cold studio space, we have room for Chuck's rage and mine to grow independently. We are aware that our negativity and bitterness stem from the alcoholic cesspool we were brought up in so we are careful not to focus this anger on each other. We are always on the verge of a disagreement over something, though.

When Chuck has his first one man-show at the FAR Gallery on Long Island, we drink to relax ourselves enough to go, smoke a little grass to loosen up and then Chuck says out of the blue, "Your nails. You don't have the polish on right. I can see white on the sides."

I go bonkers and break a few of my favorite things. When I throw a large crystal piece out the fifth floor window onto 45th Street, Chuck grabs my arm. I can't get away, but I am not afraid of him. He takes my fist and hits himself in the face with it over and over again, while I scream. When we finish our mutual fit, he has a black eye and a bruised face and my arm looks like I did a round with a welterweight. By the time we arrive at the opening, we are a horrible sight to behold. Everyone is too embarrassed to ask why we are so battered, besides it's obvious to all that I beat Chuck to a pulp. I am the abuser. I don't get any drunker at the show because my dad is there and for some reason I never drink when he's around. We invited him to the show because he loves Chuck's work. Dad takes the whole group of us to dinner afterwards. I can tell that the Shiek and Chuck like each other and that makes me happy. The show is a huge success and some of the world finally learns that Chuck is a genius.

Chuck and I continue to have some good times, good sex, good drugs. We drink lovely wines and meet beautiful creative people who become lifelong friends.

Supporting Life

I find work through a temp agency on 57th Street. On an

assignment at *Penthouse* Magazine, I meet Rosalie Muskatt. She is an instant friend even though she's a lot younger than I am. She is so smart, so wise and funny. I think she's a whole life prodigy. I make her my New York role model. Rosalie works for Patty Bosworth, the editor of *Viva* (and later *Vanity Fair*). Patty is a great writer and a former Broadway actress. Rosalie loves what she's doing, so she recommends me for a job she's not interested in with John Cassavetes at Faces International. His partner, Al Ruban, hires me without hesitation and I have a job that I enjoy for the first time. Work that isn't acting, that is. The New York office is the distribution arm for *A Woman Under the Influence* which is a pretty big hit, considering the maverick that Cassavetes is. I'm lost at Faces for a couple of days. Then Jeff Lipsky, Cassavetes' protégé, shows up one morning with coffee, donuts, energy and the answer to every film question I have.

I don't think Cassavetes knows that there are drugs being dealt out of his back office, and John doesn't care that we drink all day long while we work. He spends most of his time in Los Angeles, but when he visits New York, we all drink even more. He is a great man, actor, director, writer, producer and drinker. Al is the backbone of the company.

Aloft

Chuck and I try to stay together, to use our love constructively. He has his enormous talent to keep him going. He is already the greatest living realist painter of his time—according to his peers and many art historians. His work is his life. He wins awards. We go to openings. But money is an issue. Money and people. Weekends and nights are spent partying.

One such party is a prime example of why Chuck and I cannot stay together. Cassavetes' friend, Sam Shaw, a well-respected photographer, has another friend, an art collector who throws a party to celebrate something: a new painting, a new wife, something. Sam invites the Cassavetes crew to go with him and he says I can bring Chuck because Chuck will be blown away by the art collection. I arrange to meet Chuck at the party after work so he can spend more time there looking at the work, but I have to go home and change clothes first. I drink Tanqueray all afternoon with Blaine Novak, a young producer and co-worker. Before we realize it, it is too late to go home and change. I have on old bellbottom jeans and a tiny yellow T-shirt that says, "I could have been a contender."

There are no taxis because it's raining, so we walk the eight blocks to the party on Central Park West without umbrellas and arrive sopping wet.

Chuck sees the state I'm in and tries to get me out of there as fast as he can. He is more embarrassed and angrier than I have ever seen him. And I hear the words I am always waiting to hear.

"I can never count on you."

We don't go to parties together after that, but we drink every day and every night. He drops acid, takes speed and is unfaithful. He needs more than I can offer him. He has an acquisitive nature; he is insatiable and obsessive in all areas.

Chuck helps his friends MaryBeth McKenzie and the love of her life, Tony Mysak, rent one of the loft spaces when it becomes available in the building and I gain a lifelong friend. I have never felt so close to another woman in my adult life. MaryBeth is amazing. She is an incredible artist: hardworking, compulsive, kind, creative, and very funny. She grew up in Ohio, too, but in a real family in Lakewood.

Ups and Downs

Money is tight.

I'm learning about beauty and the appreciation of it from Chuck. And I am able to support us in exchange for this new life.

My world is at its most complete for this moment. I love. I am loved. I enjoy my work and my friends. I have stopped looking for acting work entirely.

Even though gray is still my favorite color, Chuck introduces others to me: greens, blues, purples, reds. He's all light and color and I'm not, but he loves me anyway. And I love him.

Acid. Always leery of it, I finally try it one Easter morning. Diego, the 18-year-old boy artist who is staying with us in the loft, and I—along with Jason and Chuck—drop acid. Just a little for me and none for Kees. He's a terrific artist from Amsterdam who lives in one of the lofts in our building. I trust him. He's a great friend and so he will be my guide.

Every living thing becomes spectacular. Diego is an Easter lily, Cain and Abel try to hide from me, but I can see their blood coursing through their little blue veins. After too many hours and when Kees, my guardian angel, falls asleep, I walk across town to Fifth Avenue to The Record Hunter and buy an album of French music. I walk home down the middle of empty streets and play the album in my head. I sing along, understanding French for the first time.

When I get home, still flying, Chuck and I begin a night of great sex in our cocoon. Then for me everything dies. All the brilliant colors turn brown and gray and black. The plants wither and rot. The cats are dead and lie together in sepia piles of bones. Sepia. Sleepia. I am dying. Everything is. I panic and Chuck wakes Kees up and he comes into the bedroom to help. He has Valium for me. I take the yellow pill and finally slow down enough to fall asleep. I cry all week about dying at the end of the acid trip.

Chuck and I are up one day and down the same day.

We have an agreement. I pay everything except the rent. The rent is two hundred dollars and after the first 10 months, I have to take a small loan from the Actor's Equity Credit Union to pay the rent he hasn't paid in all the time we've been together. It is not working out the way we planned. Paint, brushes, canvas and models are all very expensive. Not to mention the cost of booze and drugs. I don't understand. Chuck's work is magnificent. Chuck opens my eyes to the fact that an artist, no matter how great he is, cannot count on people buying paintings. It's a random event.

Faces

I stay at work later and later now that I am settled in at Faces. After work, Larry Shaw, and I often stop at a strip club he likes. It doesn't take too many trips there for all the girls to end up sitting with us at our table during their breaks. I'm fascinated by them; their beauty, their lives. Larry is overweight, wears glasses, takes too many drugs and loves beautiful women. He basks in the glow of the girls at the table. I'm happy to be included in their conversations and find a lot of myself in them.

However late I get home, Chuck's friends are always there, though, friends from the building, friends from his world.

At last I make an attempt to do things Chuck's way. I

invite Jeff Lipsky over after work. Sort of a goodbye party and screening because Cassavetes wants him to join the Los Angeles crew. We have a great time passing a joint around while we watch Jeff's first film.

The next week, we find out that Diego has Hepatitis and we all have to get shots. Painful shots.

Mood Swings

When I'm not feeling good about myself or about our relationship, I avoid sex. Booze and mood swings are my life.

One night when I am drunk, I leave our lair and go into the main part of the loft. I break glass and once again throw expensive crystal pieces out the open fifth floor window. I scream and cannot stop until Chuck gets my attention by screaming, too. He shakes me. I cannot stop screaming. I am out of control and we both know it's time for me to move on. He cannot cope with my moods, my outbursts or my blackouts. And I know he can't love me anymore.

And we cannot handle life and each other at the same time. I am unhappier by the second and I see his disgust for me. I don't dress the way he likes me to. I drink too much at the wrong times. I won't wear red lipstick. My cats get on his nerves and he threatens to torture them while I'm at work. On a trip back to Ohio to visit his family he falls in love with someone else. By the time I've moved out they are already planning their fairytale wedding.

I learned so much about life from Chuck, but not how to grieve quickly and move on. That is something I might never learn. I am deeply wounded and soul dead. Another failure for my list.

My last memory of Chuck is his visit to my new apartment just before he ties his second knot. We have lunch at Teacher's, get slightly drunk and make love all afternoon in my near-the-ceiling loft bed. It is the best sex we have ever had. I guess he wants me to remember him. All I want to do is forget him. And I know I never will.

Chapter 31

The Upper Westside

It's still the early 1970s. Now I'm on my own in an apartment on 85th Street between Central Park West and Columbus. It's cozy, just one large room and a bath. The kitchen is cut off from the living space by white shutters. The ceilings are high. Cain and Abel and I sleep in a loft bed high above the furniture that is crammed into the space below. The colors remind me of a cemetery because I have a grass green rug remnant now.

I'm still working at Faces, but it's slow and it's a good thing because it takes months for me to come out of my stupor. I focus on acting again to keep my wits about me. I audition. I get callbacks. I am excited all over again about acting. I finally have a commercial agent, but I also go to every open call that is posted on the Equity board. I audition for a Broadway show, *Equus*—and after five callbacks, the director has narrowed it down to two of us for the girl's role. It involves nudity, but it means working with well-known actors and I am even hopeful. In the end they choose the other actress. The one with dark hair.

This has happened to me pretty regularly, but it never hurt this much. It's often between a woman with dark hair and me. An older woman and me. Younger woman. Shorter, taller, fatter. They have no imagination and can only slot us by physical attributes. No acting ability involved in the selection. I'm devastated by each rejection as I am not built to roll with the punches, take it on the chin, or any of the other stupid phrases that are true.

Chapter 32

The Left Coast

In 1975, John Cassavetes asks Al Ruban to produce a film for him in California. Al takes me along—both of them dangling the promise of a role in the new film. The script is wonderful. Gena Rowlands and Ben Gazzara will star.

I move from New York City to Los Angeles. I have no money, no love, no desire and only east coast clothes, Cain and Abel, and the promise of a small role in a film, and a job that pays $275 a week. Cassavetes' friend/driver, Jack, picks me up at LAX and drives me directly to the Faces International Films, Inc., office. This is my training ground for a new life in the film business. It is definitely time to throw myself into someone else's work.

Cain and Abel and I are at Faces International Films in Beverly Hills just 20 minutes when an earthquake hits and the chair I'm sitting in rolls across the room. I'm ready to go back to New York. But it's too late for that now.

In some ways this is the best job I've ever had. In some ways it is the worst. As the upfront money is eaten by the production, I take on more and more responsibility. I learn much about film from Cassavetes and his crew, but the thing I learn best is that I can drink whatever is supplied free for the production. I don't have to drink just things I like. On the *Opening Night* set that means Ouzo and cheap red and white wines from the Napa Valley. We have cases of the stuff. I have a great time. Of course this is Los Angeles in the 70s, so now I have a little cocaine—supplied by one or another of the crew members—in the morning with my coffee and Quaaludes at night with my wine.

I develop a tremendous respect for Cassavetes' work ethic and the devotion of his allies. I become another one of his followers. I am on call 24-hours a day and—as I have no life of my own—it is perfect.

Working on/in this film is fun, frightening and frenzied. Gena Rowlands and John Cassavetes have beautiful children—Xan, Zoe and Nick. John tells a story one day about Xan. When she was five, she pretended he was kidnapping her and screamed out the open window of their car until the police pulled them over. This was all because she wanted to stay at her friend's house. Zoe is the quiet one. Nick is more like Gena, I think. Creative and kind. Gena is a devoted mother and she loves John as much as he loves her. And Gena has a good mother, too. I am envious of that. I should envy their fame, but it is Gena's relationship with her mother that gives me pangs. I long for that kind of love.

When I see Gena's mother, I always think about my mother. Her life seems okay now that she's been sober for a while. She had a little slip with tranquilizers, but I think that's over now, too. I think about my mother a lot. I call her every Sunday to check on her and hear about the family. I miss Darryl. I worry about him and I worry about my mother, but Leonard is taking good care of them. At least they are safe. I still have a deep sadness where my mother is concerned. I love her and am afraid for her, too. Depression is with her always. Thank god for Leonard.

Nightmare Allies

One night, I dream that John Cassavetes is Christ and I wake up in a cold sweat. He is not a god. He drinks like my mother and has my father's personality. He treats us all like children and we adore him because his entire crew is made up of waifs, orphans, abused and neglected children all grown up with nowhere to go. Faces is the creative version of the dysfunctional family I've been a part of all my life. Is this a step up?

John feels superior to many of his friends, but he loves them all. He helps the people he meets along the way, men and women he worked with on his way up. He is loyal to all the actors who aren't as talented as he is.

One crazy drunken night, he fires his entire crew. We are shooting at his house. It's the séance scene in *Opening Night* with Gena, her mother Lady Rowlands, John's mother, and Joan Blondell. He fires everyone except the actors, Richard Upper—his still photographer—and me. Who knows why besides JC? He is warm, hot, cold, loving, hating. Just the way he writes his scripts. Jumping from one feeling to another. Tonight my friend MaryBeth is visiting from New York. She's in the bar waiting for me. Later she tells me that John came by, winked at her and smiled in the middle of all his rage and said, "Hi, Sweet, can I get you a drink?"

Saint Joan

Joan Blondell plays the writer in *Opening Night*. My promised small role is Joan's assistant in the film. I am thrilled to meet Joan Blondell. An idol of mine turns out to be the kindest woman I've ever known. She has her own family demons, but she is a beautiful soul, loving and generous in all ways. And she loves her cats, a Siamese named Oui-Oui and a rescue she calls Flakey. She is shy and works hard even though arthritis causes her constant pain. She also has leukemia. She works through it all. I admire her so much. She is a strong woman.

Out of the Money

When we run out of money at Faces, John calls a friend of his who owns a posh pizza place in Beverly Hills and says, "Why don't you bring over that script you wanted me to read, and a few pizzas." He has an unlimited supply of friends who owe him favors. And vice-versa.

In this bad financial state, John takes me to a meeting at the Beverly Hills Hotel. We use my dilapidated Volkswagen bug as it's the only transportation we have at the moment. I go because he wants me to stop him from blowing up if he gets angry with them and more importantly he needs a driver. If Al were here, he would have been at this meeting, but when the money left, he had to leave, too. So John and I meet the potential backers, four of them. We share a nice breakfast in the Polo Lounge and the schmoozing begins. John doesn't want to pay them back first, he doesn't want to give them a percentage, and on and on and on.

"Come on, John. Remember we were all just poor kids from Brooklyn trying to make an honest buck?" one of the potential backers asks.

And John looks him right in the eye.

"I was never poor. I'm not from Brooklyn. Don't include me in your phony reminiscing. Just give me the money to make my film."

End of meeting.

"What good are you?" John asks me on the way out.

Chapter 33

Oh, Bobby, No Longer A Boy

"Sweetie-pie, you better get your mother and yourself to Sacto pronto." It's Bob, one of my former stepfathers, calling to tell me the latest horror story about Bobby, his son—my half-brother.

"Man, he was left for dead in the bottom of a boat by a bunch of nasty pushers," Bob says. "I told him this was going to happen one day if he kept selling, using and stealing."

On the flight to Sacramento from Los Angeles, I have a lot of time to think about Bobby. Poor Bobby.

My mother was fall-down drunk throughout her pregnancy with him in Akron in 1950. I'm reminded that one wintry night, when she was seven months pregnant, she slipped into a snowdrift outside the DAV where she and Bob hung out. She was like a turtle stuck on its back, legs in the air, until she passed out. Bob found her later, after last call. She contracted pneumonia that night and treated herself with Seagram's Seven Crown. And this is the story his dad loved to tell.

Bobby was born in City Hospital on a snowy March day. With his curly blonde hair, thick like our mother's, blue eyes like his dad's, he was nearly a poster-perfect baby except that his right foot turned in a bit, and he was saddled with braces on his little leg that forced him to clump around like Laura from *The Glass Menagerie* when he finally started walking.

A flight attendant's soft voice breaks through and catches me off-guard.

"Miss, please pull down your tray. Miss."

On my tray she places two tiny bottles of Johnnie Walker Red and a plastic cup with the single ice cube I'd requested, along with a bag of Macadamia nuts. The flight from Los Angeles to Sacramento is too long.

Half of Brother Bobby

My mind travels back in time faster than the plane moves forward. I am in third grade at King School. I'm eight, Bobby is three. Mother and Bob fail at selling Christmas trees, and end up broke. Bob is a good house painter, too, but it is always winter. Bobby and I are sent to live with my mother's uncle Raymond, his second wife Laura and his daughter, my 13-year-old cousin June.

Laura runs a baby daycare center. She takes Bobby and me in free because we are family and because we are broke and because they have an abundant sense of responsibility.

Uncle Raymond works long hours in an office at Firestone Tire and Rubber Company—a family member who is neither an idiot nor a complete drunk. Several times a year he teases me with something he thinks is funny.

"Where's my birthday present?" he asks. "Don't you know today's my birthday?"

And I cry because I have no gift for him.

"Just kidding. My birthday's not today, Silly."

Their house in West Akron is old and large and white and trimmed in dark forest green with a wraparound porch. It is in a good section of town not far from the Krispy Kreme Donut Shop. Bobby and I share a room. Cousin June is in junior high school and she becomes my ideal, my role model now because she has her own room, among other things.

King is my new favorite school. Laura encourages me to join the Brownies. They're like girl scouts only younger and they wear brown. We move back in with my mother before I get to fly up, but it was fun while it lasted. We were on the Winky Dinks TV Show once.

At Aunt Laura and Uncle Raymond's house, dinner is a new experience for me, it's a family event.

My new best friend is so rich that she rides to school in a limousine. Soon the limo is picking me up, too. One day the limo drops me off at home a little earlier than usual and I am just about to open the kitchen door when through the window, I see my Aunt Laura bang a heavy dinner plate straight down on Bobby's head.

I scream and drop my books and run to him. Bobby sits on a tall stool trying not to cry out loud. He is petrified. I put my arms around him and hold him tight. He trembles and mumbles incoherently.

"That little monster is evil. He's the devil," sweaty, deranged, wild-eyed, Laura screams.

"If you ever touch him again," I say quietly. "I will tell

everyone. Everyone. Uncle Raymond, everyone at school, and the police. Do not ever touch Bobby again. Ever."

Bobby clings to me.

"Bobby, will you tell me if she hurts you again?"

He nods his head.

Laura calms down immediately, and the nice aunt prepares dinner as usual. I can't understand why Laura is so kind to me and so cruel to Bobby.

Double Dose

"Please make sure your seats are in the upright position and that your seat belts are securely fastened."

I take a taxi straight to the hospital. My mother flew in from Ohio and is waiting for me at Bobby's dad's house, but I want to go to the hospital and see my brother first. I find his room and step inside. A man lies motionless in the bed, propped up a bit. Tubes and IVs everywhere. His face is battered, swollen, red, and his head is covered with a bandage. I go back out and check the name to make sure it's Bobby.

A nurse sees me and comes to the door.

"Angels watching over this one," she says.

I go back into the room and stand close to the bed. Bobby's mouth is wired shut. In front of him on a tray are a pencil, white notepad, and a plastic cup with a flexible straw. He is asleep. The room is warm, lights low, and I sit on an uncomfortable chair near him. I stare at this stranger. I'm tired and my head aches. And I can't stop crying.

I focus on Bobby. Then I close my eyes, and my memories take over, once more. He is four years old. I stand at the top of a long driveway. Bobby calls my dog Spike from across the street when a car is coming. Spike knows better. Bobby knows better. Spike bleeds to death on the way to the vet.

Bobby at five. He lives with his dad, and visits us. It is autumn and the leaves are falling. Cousin Michael, age six, and Bobby rake leaves all day and roll around in them. They have a great time. Then they put all the leaves into a huge cardboard box. Bobby talks Michael into climbing into the box with the beautiful red and yellow and orange dry leaves. He throws a lighted match into the box. Michael is rescued by his stepfather.

When Bobby is nine, Bob calls to tell my mother that her son burned down a neighbor's house on the way to school because they wouldn't let him walk on the grass. When he's 11, we play a game of darts when he visits Akron. He waits until I go to the board to pull mine out and he throws his darts into the back of my head. He is a good shot. Fifteen. Alcohol and heroin take over his life. I can't dredge up a single happy memory, so I open my eyes and stare at him. He looks like a punch-drunk fighter. He opens his eyes and sees me. Only then am I absolutely sure it is him. I recognize those blue eyes, as bloodshot as they are. He motions for me to hold the white pad in place on the tray while he writes, "Hey, Sis."

Chapter 34

My Kind of Guy

I return to Los Angeles, traumatized by my trip to Sacramento. Bobby will survive. My mother is not doing as well. Bob was the love of her life and seeing him again and seeing Bobby in the hospital was almost too much for her. She returns to tranquilizers and loses her job at Lerner's.

I focus on work and try to forget about my family.

An English guy named Tom is John Cassavetes' editor. He brought him from England after *"Husbands"* was filmed over there. He is nice, quiet and until I see him dead drunk, I have no interest in him at all.

On June 25th, I wait to meet Tom and his friends at The Kingshead Pub in Santa Monica to celebrate his birthday. By the time he arrives, I've had enough Watney's to loosen me up. I am nervous about parties, but I also want to be part of the group, the Faces family. Tom arrives around 10 o'clock. I yell, "surprise!" And he *is* surprised that a virtual stranger is the only one at his birthday party. We talk and sit at the bar and wait for the rest of his mates who never arrive. We close the place down and get in our cars to drive home. He's in his light blue Karmann Ghia; I am in my leased car for the production, a Pontiac something or other.

I drive home without incident. He is stopped by the police and then released.

Our first date?

Anglophilia

No surprise to anyone at Faces, Tom and I are inseparable after that one drunken birthday night. He's English, a lush with the occasional drug problem. Severely depressed and determined to stay that way, he is definitely a challenge for me. I dive in and belly-flop into his misery to avoid my own. Tom is all sadness and gentleness. I am all empathy and awkwardness. He talks to me.

His scoutmaster molested him when he was 12 and he is still sick with shame about it. His father beat him nearly to death a few times. At age six, one of the more severe beatings sent young Tom to the hospital for several weeks. He is deaf in one ear from that particular bout with good old dad. It's amazing that he's so gifted an editor, sound and picture, with hearing in only one ear.

Fortunately his older sister saved him from as much pain as she could and is his dearest friend and strongest supporter. I am her American stand-in. His mother is a lovely woman with no self-esteem who could not defend herself, let alone her two children. Not when they were children and not now. Dear old dad's name is also Tom. My Tom hates his name. He hates his dad and cringes when he hears his own name spoken aloud.

After late night drinks, he tells me other family stories.

"I loved my granddad. When he died he left me his lovely toolbox, but my dad took it away and kept it for himself. Said it was too good for a child. Too good for me, he meant."

So Tom and I stay connected by talking in spurts about being unlucky in love and in life. We both adore cats, British films, Alan Price, "*Oh, Lucky Man.*" He tells me he even named his cat Price, but changed it the day he got him because the little kitten ran into the street in front of his Westwood apartment and was hit by a car. Tom spent a bloody fortune to fix him up good as new. Forever after he is known as Pricey. But the very best thing for me is that Tom has a little girl named Emma. She's five and in England with her mum, Tom's ex-wife. I start planning for a visit immediately. He doesn't want to visit England, so I rattle on forever about Emma coming to visit us. It takes a while.

After a couple of months of what we laughingly think of as dating, we rent an apartment in Hermosa Beach. Not long after that, we persuade my brother Darryl to leave Akron and try Los Angeles for a bit. I am ecstatic when he moves in with us.

When Tom finally accepts that Cassavetes is not going to come through and help him get his green card, we pick up a marriage license downtown, get our blood drawn by Gena's doctor in Beverly Hills, and shove all that information—along with divorce papers from our prior marriages—into the glove compartment of his Karmann Ghia. Then we head toward Palm Springs. As we speed along the highway, Tom mentions casually.

"You know one thing about you I really hate? You laugh too much and quite loudly. I'm not used to that sort of thing. And you have too bloody many friends."

"Sod off," I reply with my best English accent.

I learned something from Lionel Bart after all.

Tom drives faster and faster after my "sod off" comment. I notice for the first time that Tom is a lousy driver. Then we hear the siren. The Banning County speeding ticket for going 50 miles over the limit should have told us something.

We travel the rest of the way in silence.

I think about my brother Darryl back at our apartment taking care of Cain, Abel and Pricey. He is undecided about what to do next, but he is alive and determined to escape from the Ohio life. He's 19, intelligent, handsome, and he already knows a lot about life. I relate to it all and know his life will get better after he's in California for a while. Darryl can do anything he wants to do. And he loves Los Angeles.

Tom's stony silence gives me way too much mind wandering time.

I think about my dad in intensive care at Kings County Hospital in Brooklyn. Last week he suffered a massive coronary and his heart is too damaged for a bypass.

And Cassavetes, my hero, has cirrhosis and continues to drink and work like a demon. He had hepatitis once and that made him even more susceptible to liver problems.

Just Desert

We reach the Spa Hotel and check in, still without speaking to one another. We start drinking right away. We drink like we've been lost in the desert for days. We argue. Then just talk. Marriage yes. Marriage no. We treat it like some kind of game. The "Lost in the Desert" game.

I need a partner and a friend. I'm tired of being alone. I love Tom and want to save this battered lost boy. Exhausted from bickering, and woozy from emptying all those little bottles in the mini-bar, we escape into sleep in our separate king-size beds.

In the morning, with slightly clearer heads, we decide not to marry.

"Sorry I was so obnoxious yesterday."

I get no response from my sunbather and husband to be who is on the lounge chair next to mine by the pool.

Instead of a wedding we have deep-tissue massages, hot mineral baths and facials. I stay in the over-heated Jacuzzi until

I'm crimson and think the top of my head is about to burst into flames.

Late in the afternoon we return to our room to shower and then start out for an early dinner at Hamburger Hamlet, just up the block. We clean up nicely. I put on an expensive off-white silk blouse and over-priced taupe-colored trousers. He wears jeans and a pale blue silk shirt.

"My stomach isn't doing so well. Let's not go to the Hamlet."

"We look too good for Hamburger Hamlet, anyway," he whispers through his teeth.

We both forget the name of the really good restaurant someone told us about and drive around hoping we might recognize it if we pass it. In our search we find an old mission called Unity in the Desert—where Reverend Batesole marries us. He utters a few beautiful words of no particular denomination, and we are husband and wife. Marriages number two for both of us. It's the 70s and even though the two saintly-looking women in their late 80s stare disapprovingly at our wedding attire, they are our witnesses. One of them continues to knit while she watches the ceremony. I wish I could knit.

And then I hear the words, "Tom, you may kick your bride."

I know that can't be it because my new husband leans over and kisses me ever so delicately.

Tom looks almost happy. I must be happy, too.

On the way back to our hotel, we stop at Saks Fifth Avenue and I charge two delicate Baccarat champagne flutes on my Amex card. This necessitates our second stop at the liquor store where I charge two bottles of *Dom Perignon*. One for Tom and one for me.

Back in our room, we drink to our health, England, Manhattan, the film business, marriage and friendship, our future, the future. And then we return to the liquor store for two more bottles of bubbly. We swill champagne until we pass out on one king-size bed.

We spend our first full day of wedded bliss recovering from deadly hangovers. We have our massages, the saunas and then frozen Margaritas by the pool. It is December sixth. We fry beneath the late afternoon sun. Words to a song I like keep running through my head.

I went to the desert on a horse with no name.

"Reverend Batesole was wonderful, wasn't he, Tom?"

Tom half smiles, without opening his eyes.

We pack for our return to reality. I look at the white suit I had bought for my wedding. What a waste of money. I'll never wear it now unless I'm buried in it.

Chapter 35

Back to Faces

Out of respect and loyalty, we work for Cassavetes as long as we can afford to, until he runs out of money and can't pay Tom or me anymore. We have bills to pay, rent, credit cards. *Opening Night* is in the editing stage, so I take another job at Taft Entertainment in Westwood where I read scripts, wear a skirt every day for the first time in my adult life and cater to the CEO. He is an alcoholic and drinks scotch all day long. He is a good and thoughtful man living in another time.

Our marriage is a lonely, unhappy time for me and yet I grow more dependent upon and responsible for Tom every day. Our sex life is nil. He is neither affectionate nor demonstrative and I feel that when we try to make love, he is not there. He makes no sounds during sex. Deathly quiet. I am intimidated into being quiet, too, as if there is someone in the next room listening to us. I can't even try after a while and so we grow further apart. I love him in so many ways, but I have no skills to use to get through to him.

The people in Hermosa Beach with their Christmas trees made from empty beer cans begin to get on our nerves, so we move to the *Chateau des Fleur* in Hollywood. We renovate, redo, redecorate, rescue a kitten, furnish with depression-era furniture—but nothing makes us happy. Darryl likes Hermosa and stays there when we move back to Los Angeles.

So then we move again—this time into the Hollywood Hills. We have a beautiful apartment in a 1920s deco triplex. Our neighbors are two gay couples who are nothing but kind and welcoming. We celebrate our good fortune by drinking more and more and more.

We finally have enough credit available on my cards to go to New York so Tom can meet my dad and then to Akron to meet my mother and Leonard.

"I would never have married you if you'd introduced me to them before we got married."

I think he's kidding.

"I'm not kidding. They're all mad, completely mad."

"My mother loves you," I tell him. And she does.

Tom continues editing for Cassavetes. I hate my job at Taft where I am now reading police procedurals every day and writing the occasional synopsis. I miss the true insanity of the Faces office. I miss drinking all day. Cassavetes resents me for leaving even though he knows I have to make money to live. He cools toward me. He and Tom cut me out of *Opening Night*, except for a few moments here and there where Joan Blondell made it impossible for me to be cut from the scene. My husband and my hero cutting me to bits in a dark room in Beverly Hills is an image that stays for a long, long time. I ask Tom for the outtakes to make a reel and he forgets to get them for me.

And Unto Us a Child

In the summer Tom's little girl, Emma, comes to visit us. She changes my life forever and is the highpoint of all my times with Tom. I adore Emma. Amazing and brilliant Emma. She is beautiful and clever, everything I'd ever wanted in a child. I take time off from work to take care of her, while Tom focuses on a paying job sound editing a movie of the week at Paramount. We take her shopping, to the zoo, Sea World, Disneyland, anywhere she wants to go. The beach is her favorite. She loves the sea, after all she is still English, even if she is just six. Little Emma Jane. Tom loves Emma so much and when I see this side of him I love him more.

When Emma goes home to England, Tom and I are completely lost. We try to stay together, but our emptiness echoes through the tiny tree house we end up buying in Silver Lake.

Chapter 36

New Yo-Yo-York

In 1982, in an effort to save my sanity and in order to drink without driving, I move back to New York and find a job through the classified section of *The New York Times*. I'll be doing research for Garson Kanin and Ruth Gordon. They are amazing. Miss Gordon is a genuine character. He is more outgoing and wears Chanel No. 5, but I keep my distance.

While looking through a file one day for something or other, I find a story Gar wrote entitled, "I Wished Her Dead and Wished Her Dead Until One Day I Died." Maybe the happiness I'm seeking, even the love, does not exist.

Breathing Lessons

When in doubt, I always go back to my first love. Acting. I sign up for a Shakespearean class at a lovely little place at the back of St. John the Divine, the magnificent Episcopal Church uptown on Amsterdam. The class—called Potter's Field—is all about breathing. Breathing is something I've never really done right. It is freeing and I actually believe I might try acting again when I get a few dollars together.

One day in New York, I spot Cassavetes on the other side of Madison Avenue talking on a payphone. I sneak up behind him to surprise him. He hugs me and hands me the phone.

"Hello?"

"Hello, Gar?"

We laugh so hard. He's on the phone with Garson Kanin. What a funny world. Neither John nor Garson can believe I went through *The Times* when they were close friends all the time. John and Ruth Gordon were in *Rosemary's Baby* together and have been close ever since.

My job is on 57th Street and I live at 104th and Broadway where I spend my time with Cain and Abel in our nearly empty room—a borrowed bed and a borrowed table with a borrowed chair—in the dark again. I drink at home alone—wine or Asahi beer—and broil a chicken breast and tear some lettuce for a salad. Then I stare out the window into the alleyway. There is nothing to see. The cats could have told me that. They sit there all day long hoping something will fly by. Maybe someday I will.

I call my mother almost every night after I've had a couple of glasses of whatever. She tries to talk some sense into me. "Go back to Tom and get over this acting thing. Nobody's happy. The kind of happiness you're looking for does not exist."

Tom and I also talk on the phone almost every day. I begin to miss him and to forget how painful it is to be with him. I pack up poor Cain and Abel again and return to Tom and Los Angeles to stab at our marriage, again.

Chapter 37

Family Therapy

Just before I pick up the phone to call Dr. Dan, I think back to how fortunate I am to have him as my psychiatrist.

I remember one evening at dusk in Beverly Hills, sometime in the 1980s. Naomi, my therapist, paces back and forth in her beautifully designed, professionally decorated office. I stare out the window without seeing and wait for her to say something. She is as warm and compassionate a psychologist as I've ever met and I feel blessed that she sees me.

"Your problems are beyond my capabilities."

She hands me two stark white business cards. One for a man and one for a woman. Both psychiatrists.

"Would you rather see a man or a woman?"

"I don't care."

It's not a massage, I think, and wish I could disappear. I look at the cards more closely. I choose the man hoping that will hurt Naomi in some tiny way.

At the end of our last quiet session, I stand to leave and she hugs me. I hug her back. This has always been one of my most dreaded fears. that no one could help me. I do not care when someone leaves me. Being banished hurts.

I smile, thank her, and turn around to face her at the door.

"You're sending me to Encino you know."

I make an appointment and the following week I take the 101 to Encino, park underground and hope the bozo validates.

I am afraid of freeways, high-rises, elevators and the valley.

I step out of the elevator at the 19th floor, turn right, then right, and then left. It's a bloody maze. I walk as slowly as possible down the long and sterile corridor. On my journey, out of mindless curiosity, I open an unnumbered closet door to my left and look inside. I see me. I am hanging from a noose, neck broken, feet dangling, color drained. I slam that door and rest with my back against it for a few moments until I catch my breath.

There are dark double doors at the end of the hallway.

On the other side of the doors, I am alone in the large waiting room, staring at the array of magazines and a collection of framed abstract art. I am judging him. The doctor. I can't help myself. Everything is beige, bloody beige. If he's such a good doctor, shouldn't he recognize that something is ugly? I give him the benefit of the doubt. This is just the waiting room. He shares it with several other psychiatrists. The magazines are good and current.

I see some buttons and get up to punch the one above his name. The door opens immediately, which stuns me.

He reaches out to me and shakes my hand.

"Running late, be with you momentarily."

The door closes. *Momentarily.* I hate to wait. After a few minutes, I organize the magazines. *Rolling Stone* with *Rolling Stone*, *New Yorker* with *New Yorker*, *Parents* with *Parents*, *Westways* with *Westways*, and then by date.

The door opens.

"Come in."

I force some kind of smile and feel myself shrinking. He holds the door open saying nothing about how tidy the magazines look. He is twice my height, slender, nice looking. We both have on gray sweaters and trousers and turtlenecks. I wonder if he changed clothes to make me feel at ease.

He breaks into my thoughts.

"Where would you like to sit?"

I look out the window. He sits at his desk and I choose the couch.

"I am a psychotherapist not a psychoanalyst. If you want to lie down, though, do so by all means."

He swivels his chair to face me and puts his feet up on a small footstool.

"Bad back."

"I'm sorry."

"No need to be. I'm fine. The footstool helps. Naomi told me a little about you."

I sit stiffly on the couch. A ficus tree branch with too many leaves hangs above me. I chose my spot. I will not move. I stare past him to the empty beige wall behind and begin to cry. I hate to cry. I hate to cry. He hands me a box of tissues. I cry until I can barely breathe and have to use my asthma inhaler. He is the one who can help me. I feel it in my bones and I am horrified.

"Tell me a little about your family," he finally says.

Here we go again. I continue to stare over his shoulder at the wall behind him. But before I can start my unhappy childhood tale, the blank beige wall splits down the middle, like the Red Sea parting, or a seven-point-two earthquake.

A beautifully designed, life-size vaudeville stage appears, lights and all. I look past and through the doctor to a skinny little girl in a satiny yellow costume who tap dances onstage and up to an easel at stage left where she places an elaborate placard that is almost as big as she is. It reads: *Juggle and Hide.* The little girl smiles, curtsies, and winks at me. She taps all the way across the stage and then back again. She stands still and points to the placard as thick velvety gold curtains descend.

The wall is a wall again.

The doctor asks gently, "What is it? Where are you right now?"

I tell him the vaudeville story, figuring if I'm going to get anything out of this therapy thing and save my life, he might as well come all the way into my head.

"I guess that sums up your childhood pretty well, according to my notes from Naomi. Juggle and hide."

I cry again. He points to the tissues.

"This is going to be expensive for both of us," I blubber.

"How so?"

"You'll be buying a lot of tissues."

We sit in silence.

He is the one to break it first.

"Is there anything going on in your life right now that you'd like to tell me about?"

I clutch his card and stare at it instead of looking at him.

"May I call you Dr. Dan?"

He nods.

"What's the initial B stand for in your name?
Bertolt."

He takes over the interaction.

"You're married?"

"Yes."

"Tell me a little about that."

"Tom. He's a film editor. English. We are both miserable. Have been for 10 years. Off and on. We have no sexual relationship at all."

"Your choice or his?"

"Mine, now. But I love him in some weird brotherly way."

An even longer silence. I get uncomfortable and fidgety.

"Last week, I woke up in the middle of the night. I was lying on my left side close to the edge of the bed facing the window. Tom was masturbating, rubbing up against my back and using his index finger to make slow wet circles on my breast around my erect right nipple."

I stop talking. Suddenly blank.

"You have a beautiful view of the valley."

"What did you do when you realized what Tom was doing?"

"Nothing. I stayed very still and let him finish. I wanted to chop him up into little pieces and feed him to our dog."

"Do you have children?"

"No, we have four cats and a new puppy named Blanche. But Tom has a beautiful little girl named Emma. She lives in England with her mum. Spends summers with us. Calls me her wicked stepmother. Says I'm mad as a hatter. I adore her."

"What about work?" Dr. Dan asks.

"Production. That's where I met Tom. We worked for the same director."

"That must be exciting."

"Not really. Did you see *Apocalypse Now?*"

"Loved it."

Blade Runner?

"Loved it."

"Children."

"Yes."

"Do you know any tennis pros?" I ask.

"Why do you ask?"

"Last night I dreamed I met you. But I was wrong; it wasn't you. He was different. Shorter. Sandy-haired. Wearing tennis clothes."

There is a long silence while Dr. Dan turns to his desk and writes out an appointment card. He turns back to me.

"My brother's your sandy-haired tennis pro. OK, let's end for today."

He hands me the appointment card. I take it without looking at it.

"Is this a good time for you?"

"I wouldn't call it a real good time."

He laughs at my stupid comment. I love that he laughs. He appreciates my humor. I can see him again.

"Saturdays at 10 o'clock. Do you know why Naomi sent you to me?"

"She hates me?"

"I treat post-traumatic stress victims at the VA Hospital, teach at UCLA and I'm a psycho-pharmacologist."

Dr. Dan walks me to the door. He holds the door open and I turn and look up at his face.

"Tom is my second husband."

I leave and walk down the same bland corridor toward the elevators. On the way, I stop and open the door I had opened earlier. There's nothing in that closet but a maze of telephone wires.

Chapter 38

The Guilt

Now that I'm back in Los Angeles, I miss New York. I love a man who loathes me more each day. Tom's words echo in my head after he falls asleep at night.

"I blame you for this. You had sex with everyone else. Why not me? What's wrong with you? Making love to you is like being with a dead person."

Dr. Dan says, "Tom is passive-aggressive."

Again And An End

By the final months of our marriage, Tom I are only capable of having dinner together and drinking until we become quiet or loud, depending on the evening, and then passing out. He drinks at work with his friends and I worry about his driving home drunk—never thinking that I am driving drunk, as well. To further separate us, Tom smokes grass day and night. Sleep is my salvation.

And then John Cassavetes dies from cirrhosis. Instead of quitting drinking, myself, I go on a spiritual quest: yoga, psychics, eccentric ministers, and meditation. I ration myself. Two or three drinks an evening, no drinking during the day except on weekends.

Tom continues to work as a sound editor. He is nominated for and wins Emmys and other editorial awards. They mean nothing to him. He places his trophies and awards on the mantle and lets our new rescue cat, Mac, who is stone deaf knock them to the bricks below one by one until they are all misshapen and funny looking.

Tom works less and less and I take a job at The Mark Taper Forum Theatre downtown at the Music Center. I am Gordon Davidson's second assistant. He's the artistic director. It is at the Taper that I really cut back on my drinking. Except for Gordon, the entire staff drinks a lot and all the time.

Dr. Dan encourages me or enables me to concentrate on myself by taking yet another acting class. I find Allen Garfield's group. They work in a small theatre in Beverly Hills—aptly named The Actor's Shelter. Offstage I am terrified.

Onstage I have a new awareness of who I am. I'm not happy with that, but the class is good even if Allen is a tough director. I trust him because he has always been one of my favorite actors. Many talented people are in the class, including pre-stardom Quentin Tarantino. He's a good actor and a great addition to the class. And what a workout we get with Allen. Dr. Dan is right again. This is an essential outlet for my pain and anger.

I love Tom and I leave him to be with me. I'm not leaving to be with someone else and that is something that Tom cannot understand.

Geographic

Before I can move far away from Tom and our little tree house, I rent an apartment nearby and take Cain and Abel with me. I am hoping this will make the transition less painful. It does not.

Then a homeless black cat shows up on my doorstep with three kittens. I find homes for the feral little ones and keep the mom. I name her Kitsch. Before I can kiss Los Angeles goodbye—again—Abel dies of kitty AIDS. It's just Cain and Kitsch and me on that flight back to New York. It's 1990 and I am lost again. Maybe a little less lost, but no less alone.

I am sick with guilt for leaving Tom, so he and I are on the phone every night until, just before we hang up one night, he says, "I hope you walk in front of a bus and get run over and die."

On January 23, 1990, Tom is pulled over by a state trooper on the Ventura Freeway for driving while dead drunk and in the wrong direction—facing the oncoming traffic. He goes to jail for the night. He joins AA. I am happy for him. About AA. He will be fine or at least better now. He is safe at last.

My love for New York is intact however much I hate myself. Rain. Shine. Snow. Heat. I love it from Battery Park to Hell's Kitchen to Morningside Heights. Theatres, cinemas, restaurants, bars, ice skating rinks, bridges. I can walk up and down across Manhattan all day long. Central Park is heaven. Shakespeare, the Carousel, Sheep's Meadow, the Fountain and the River Café, even Maxwell's Plum before they gaudied it up. Bicycling, just walking, leaves in autumn, blizzards in winter. One true love. I fell in love at six when my dad took me on the grand tour. Circle Line to the Statue of Liberty, Chinatown, Little Italy, the Upper Westside, Harlem, 42nd Street. What I do on my own in my favorite city is unforgivable—I vomit all over my city. Because no matter how little I think I drink, I still get sick.

Chapter 39

My Bottom

Monkey brain. White knuckling. Suicidal ideation. Hallucinations. Some nights I open my eyes and my studio apartment is a high-ceilinged ballroom filled with extraordinary people in elegant costumes from some other time and some other place. I watch them dance. I don't recognize anyone and I am not afraid. It's not as if they can see me. I go back to sleep, wondering if this is a dream. I awaken again, and they're still dancing.

I'm 45, and it's dead cold in New York in February 1990. I ran from Tom and Los Angeles and now I think I can take care of my problems alone, that I don't need him or Dr. Dan or anyone but my cats and a few pieces of thrift shop furniture, that I'll be fine, in time.

Eventually the dancers in my head move out of my apartment. One night not long after the costume ball, I wake up and the blank white wall at the foot of my bed is covered with hieroglyphics from ceiling to floor. I fall asleep trying to decode the ancient message. The message returns night after night, but the blank wall returns each morning.

I keep a flashlight and a notepad by my bed now. Tonight I copied some of the hieroglyphics. I plan to decipher this message.

Is this what it's like to stop drinking? Is this cold turkey? Am I having DTs? Do I ask anyone about this or go to a doctor? No. I assume it will all go away or I'll stop caring that it's happening.

Not long after Tom's escapade on the Ventura Freeway and his subsequent membership in Alcoholics Anonymous, I decide to stop drinking, too—even though I'm so many miles away from him.

First I cut down to just two drinks a day. Two Asahi beers. I shop for them each day as if they are gold. I drink them slowly each night. I am proud of myself. I am not an alcoholic. Then I cut down to one and then to none.

Although I've sent lovers, husbands and friends to AA, I will not go myself. I know everything about getting sober and

I don't need to sit around in rooms with strangers. I can do that at home. How hard can it be? After all I stopped smoking grass, using coke, taking illegal prescription drugs without much of a problem. Of course, I had alcohol to carry me through those deprivations.

To pay rent and bills, I work part-time.

I have a few friends to rely on who can still bear to be around me while I wallow in this deep depression, who can still listen to my denial and disillusionment. I can't and won't tell everyone about my nights with the dancers and the ancient messages. But my friends know my heart is broken and that I am nearly broke financially and spiritually, as well. They say I'm bereft. A word I've always liked.

An old friend, Milburn Mehlhop, a writer, actor and graphic artist, spends as much time with me as he can. He comforts me, has dinner with me. I ask him to marry me. In his wisdom he tells me he will not, that he cannot.

I begin long distance telephone therapy with Dr. Dan on a weekly basis. I will not live this life alone.

MaryBeth McKenzie

MaryBeth McKenzie remains my closest friend. She lives in that same loft building where I lived with Chuck in the 70s.

I become involved in her new desire to have a child and wander with her to fertility clinics and discuss the endless possibilities of her new obsession. I love sharing in her quest. I love children, and accept I will never have them because I am afraid. I am afraid they might turn out like my mother or father or me. Maybe I wouldn't be a good mother. I don't know.

But it is almost as exciting for me as it is for MaryBeth when she adopts two little Hungarian sisters from an orphanage near Budapest. Her life changes forever and for the better. I see very little of her after she moves into the fulltime adventure of motherhood. MaryBeth is a good mother, but she doesn't understand alcoholism. She does not think I am an alcoholic.

"Just have a glass of wine once in a while with dinner."

Because of a new and intense inward journey, my stomach takes over my life. I find a gastroenterologist in a posh office at Central Park West and 62nd Street. Since I still have my insurance via Tom and his union, I can see him. My diagnosis: inflammatory bowel disease, spastic colon, irritable colon, ulcerative colitis and diverticulitis. Dr. Griffin helps me, but right after my second colonoscopy, he is arrested for molesting patients during procedures. All my records go with him as evidence. I was so far under with Demerol during my tests that I have no idea whether or not I was one of the abused patients. I assume not so I won't have to wallow in that one, too. Although, I remember coming out from under Demerol with the doctor carrying me from the procedure room to the recovery room.

His face was close to mine.

"You are having a bad reaction to the Demerol," he whispered.

I vomited all over him.

I have only two cats in New York with me, just like the old days. Cain and Kitsch. Cain doesn't look so good, but he hangs on and I hang on. He is a big part of my life. Eighteen years is my longest relationship and it is with my Siamese cat.

Tom is sober now because he wants to be. He is coming for a visit soon. So I call the AA hotline and get the times and addresses of local meetings. I check one out for him and while sitting at the meeting and listening to the speaker, I have some kind of revelation about myself. I need meetings, too. Maybe I can live, too. Maybe I don't have to think about drinking all the time.

Tom does not visit and I get sober by going to those meetings. September 9, 1991. My sobriety date. How could I have known that I didn't have to drink? No one ever told me. I am so excited that I call my mother. She laughs, "So now you're an alcoholic, too."

I work part-time as a researcher for the smartest woman in the world and her husband who witness the ups and downs of my newfound sobriety. I go to meetings on my lunch hour. I never tell them I'm a recovering alcoholic, but I assume they know.

My Leonardo

Leonard has a heart attack in his doctor's office one day and they rush him to the hospital for a triple bypass. After that he is never well again, never the same, never happy, always afraid. The blood they give him during the surgery is tainted and he doesn't know it. Doesn't know that he will never recover.

He has only my mother, his beloved Kathleen, to look after him, to nurse him back to health. She is incapable of taking care of him.

I talk to him on the phone almost every night after his surgery, but I cannot allay any of his fears. His biggest fear is the idea of leaving my mother alone. I think she will be fine, that maybe she will even learn to live a little bit. Leonard knows better.

One day I get that dreaded phone call. "Leonard is dead." It is my mother's voice on the other end of the phone.

"I was down in the basement sorting through some clothes and I heard pounding up in the bathroom. Then there was some screaming. I thought I heard him call my name."

"What did you do then, Mother?"

"Well, I finished sorting through the clothes and put in a load of laundry and went upstairs."

"Well?"

"Well, what?"

"He was dead. Sitting on the toilet dead. He looked strange. He had some long thing hanging down by his penis. He looked something awful."

"Then what did you do?"

"I put some pajamas on him so he wouldn't be naked when they came for him. Then I called 411 or maybe it was 911."

"Don't worry. I'll call Darryl and we'll be there before you know it.

I arrive first. Darryl will be in Akron in a couple of days.

So I begin the process of burying Leonard. I meet with a mortician at Eckard's funeral home. Turns out that the building that used to be the Disabled American Veterans Club—the DAV where my mother once worked—is now a part of the mortuary that had been next door. It is where my mother first met Leonard. I had been there many times when it was a bar.

The family plot that my grandmother saved her pennies for so many years ago now adds Leonard to the group. He joins my mother's mother—Mom—and my grandma and grandpa at Rose Hill Cemetery. That leaves one empty plot available for my mother when she dies.

I didn't know how loved Leonard was until the funeral. So many friends and co-workers pay their respects while my mother sits in a daze in her Liz Claiborne black dress from the May Company. Michael and Michi are there. Everyone in the family shows up. Leonard would have loved all the perfect white roses.

On the way to the cemetery with Darryl and me, Mother flirts with the young limousine driver and points out boutiques where we can go shopping, later.

Darryl and I stay with her for a few days after the funeral. She wants to shop and sleep and seems to take Leonard's death far too well. Maybe I just want her to seem all right so I can go back to New York. Darryl stays on.

As soon as I get back to New York, I realize how out of touch with reality my mother is, so I call Darryl and ask him to let me know when he's going home, and I'll turn around and return to Akron. I had no idea how much Leonard did for my mother. Now I am starting to get the picture.

Just Mommy and Me

I go back to Akron for a little while, just till I can sort things out. The very first morning that I'm back at my mother's house, an explosion shocks me awake. Before I can think about what it is, I call 911—and then I awaken my mother. She's wearing flannel pajamas and a terry cloth robe. On the way out of the house, she stops and opens the basement door. There is another—even louder—explosion. I close the basement door and literally force her out of the house and into her car. I drive down to the corner and leave her in the car while I run back to meet the fire fighters. They douse the flames quickly and tell us how grateful we should be to be alive.

My mother is not upset at all by any of this. When we are both back in the basement with the firefighters. One of them tells us an old can of Easy-off oven cleaner ignited somehow and caused the explosion. "You girls are real fortunate. That can was too near the pilot light on the dryer."

Maintenance people put the basement back together within a few days and I escape to my life, to New York.

I call every night to see how she is doing on her own.

"I'm just fine. You don't have to call me every night."

"I love you, Mother."

"Do you?"

She is so pitiful, so sad, but I am still living on planet denial. I think that she will be better after grieving her losses. Her mother (Mom) and sister (Aunt Pat) died during the same year as Leonard. She must be in shock. She laughs inappropriately a lot and when I ask about her psychiatrist, she swears to me she's still going every week and has the pills to prove it.

My cousin Michael helps arrange for a cleaning woman and both she and my mother promise to check in with me after every visit. My cousins, nice neighbors and my mother's psychiatrist, who has my phone number and Darryl's, are all aware that she is spiraling downward.

Darryl is doing well. He's working and has friends and I am thrilled for him. There are times that I feel that he is my son. Not just my half-brother. I have to be careful not to be too controlling. He is a gift and I am grateful to have him in my life.

Back in New York my boss and her husband fire me because I stayed so long in Akron after Leonard's funeral. In their defense, I am their only employee and they need someone who can be there every day. How can they understand what I am going through? I don't understand it. I accept my dismissal as some sort of punishment that I've deserved all my life.

A Desire to Stop Thinking

I go to an AA meeting every day. I speak to no one. I arrive late and leave early. But I am not drinking and feeling better, so I figure it doesn't really matter that I am antisocial. The slogans irritate me. The people frighten me. They are either over-the-top happy or on the verge of suicide. Even when the room is crowded, no one sits next to me. I am left to suffer on my own. It is the best thing for me. I listen and learn and realize I don't have to do anything but not drink. The one message I get is that I do not have to drink. And I am supremely grateful to be rid of my hangovers.

After three months of not even nodding at anyone, I meet an interesting looking woman named Ursula, who appears to be about my age. So far all the drunks I've seen have been tall. She is short. I say hello, and she tells me there is a beginner's meeting upstairs from the meeting I've been attending so faithfully. I go upstairs at the Y with her and find a bit of a home there. I don't feel any more comfortable, but the people seem more open, honest and real and more desperate to stay sober.

At one of my meetings, after I laugh out loud at another alcoholic's remark—and no one else does—she introduces herself. She's a beautiful young woman who helps me to not drink by making me laugh and by having lunch with me nearly every day at an outdoor restaurant on Columbus Avenue. We are two complete messes. Then I hear at a meeting that when we put down the drink we return to the age when we began drinking before we can move on into maturity. For me this is true. I am the self-indulgent child now that I never got to enjoy being. I go to a meeting every day; I take all the suggestions and follow the Twelve Steps. To my amazement, I stop thinking about killing myself every waking minute of every day. I have no pink cloud, no instant relief from wanting to drink, but I go to meetings and little by little by very little my life gets better.

After my dear cat Cain dies at age 19, an old friend from Chuck and the loft days dies, too, and leaves me his gray cat, Minnie the Mooch.

Kitsch, Minnie and I move from the solitary abode on West 56th into a two bedroom pre-war apartment with my old friend from the 60s, Rick Northcutt. When we were in our mid-20s we made a pact that if we were on our own in our 40s, we'd move in together and share a large apartment. So life is good. We both love art deco and *moderne* and it's fun being with him. We don't do a lot of things together; he's busy at work and has a lot of good friends. He dates from time to time, but the guys he likes all end up being lovers first, then good friends—which, if you ask me, says a lot about what a great person Rick is. And I love him for being such a good friend and especially for learning to live with two cats and a woman. He's a dog person, after all.

Amends

When I finally work my way through some of my ancient anger and reach the AA step where you make amends to those you've harmed, I pick up the phone and track down JJ. He lives in Poughkeepsie New York, has two children, and is divorced for the third time. He drives into the city and we have lunch at Capricci's while I openly admit to my share in the demise of our marriage. He is still beautiful.

"Do you mind if I have a drink, Lovely?"

"Go ahead."

"I don't know how you do it. I know I couldn't."

But I tell him I'm sorry for not being there for him, not knowing how to be a wife. We talk for hours. I have nothing but compassion for the boy he was and the man he is. I listen. When we say goodbye back at my apartment, I feel that I will never see him again. He is lucky to be alive, too.

Job Hunting

I still have no income and am living off my credit cards.

A friend mentions Woody Allen is looking for a new assistant, so I ask Howard Fast—a great writer that I worked for back in Los Angeles in the 80s—to please get me an interview. They're friends and live in the same building on Fifth Avenue. Howard has no trouble arranging it for me. I arrive early and a young woman takes me to a screening room in Woody Allen's apartment and asks me to wait. So I wait. And wait. Suddenly he enters from behind a curtain. I hand him my résumé. We stand facing each other. He reads the résumé. I stare at him. We are dressed alike. I am mortified. I should have worn a skirt. Anyway, he asks me what my last job was like and I say, without thinking, I did research for the smartest woman in the world and helped monitor an artificial heart experiment. He laughs out loud. He doesn't hire me, but I make him laugh.

I continue to pay my bills with my credit cards.

Chapter 40

Qualification

"My name is Sharon and I am an alcoholic. It's my job to tell other alcoholics what it was like then, what happened and what it's like now."

Here I sit at a Beginners Meeting in front of about 50 newly-sober drunks. My hands shake as I take off my glasses so I won't be able to see their faces. My mouth opens and words spill out, but I have no idea what I'm saying.

"Blackouts were just delicious chocolate cakes when I was six. I think I was born alcoholic, that I was an alcoholic waiting for my first drink from the day I opened my eyes. My first drunk was New Year's Eve 1957. I stood naked in the shower with a champagne bottle and a champagne glass drinking the New Year in alone. I got sick. I didn't realize it then, but I blacked out. I was 11 going on 12.

"The thing that finally forced me to stop drinking—aside from depression and loneliness—was the blacking out.

"I remember sitting on a stoop of a brownstone uptown on the eastside of Manhattan. My last conscious awareness was a posh gallery opening several blocks from the stone-cold stoop.

"I looked at the man next to me, at the brown bag in his hand. He smiled a toothless smile and passed the bag to me. I took a sip and passed it back to him."

'Thank you. I have to go now,' I said.

'What's your hurry?' he replied.

"Plato's Retreat was a brown out, I guess, because I remember most of it. Another hideous memory. I am waiting for a bus on Broadway across from Lincoln Center. A guy starts talking to me, an English tourist it turns out. He wants to go to Plato's Retreat and they won't let him in without an escort, a woman.

'Please. Just go in with me. Then you can leave and do whatever you want. I'll pay you 50 dollars. True to his word he leaves me at the door inside Plato's Retreat. I stand there with two white towels and a 50-dollar bill. It's July 4, 1976.

America's birthday. I must have walked out of a fantastic rooftop party where we drank and cheered and sang along with Liza Minelli while we watched the tall ships sail the Hudson. And here I am at the notorious Plato's Retreat. I wander around in my white pleated knee-length shorts and blue T-shirt with a red cardigan tied around my shoulders looking every bit the bozo I am. Sneakers, I'm wearing sneakers. Everyone else is naked. There are couples seated around the pool talking, kissing, touching. The pool is full of swimmers, laughing and splashing and talking swimmers. No one pays any attention to me so I find the bar, but it is only a juice bar.

'Don't you think you're a little out of place here, missy? Why don't you go home where you belong?'

'I'll have an orange juice, please?'

"I walk around trying not to appear drunk. I find a pay phone and call MaryBeth. The phone is outside a closed room and while she coaxes me to leave, we listen to the moans coming from behind the doors."

'I promise I'll leave now. As soon as I can find my way out.'

"I run into my English host and the beautiful woman he has found. They are both naked and looking quite spectacular."

'Love, we're going to her place. Want a ride uptown or wherever?'

"They dress and I wait at the front door for them. In the cab, the beautiful woman talks to me."

'I teach special ed. Autistic kids. If you'd like to join us at my place, you'd be more than welcome.'

"Okay, so New York was mostly brownouts. But I had a lot of blackouts, too, but the worst times were after I went back to Los Angeles. I think my most frightening blackout was the day after a party in Bel Air. I remember going. Being uncomfortable. Not knowing many people. And I remember drinking as much as I could to make me able to be there, to stay there. The next thing I know, it's morning and I am home in my own bed in Hollywood. There's a wadded up paper towel full of dried blood on the floor. I shower and find that I'm not cut so it's not even my blood. I run outside. I don't see my Volkswagen bug. I think I might have run over someone. Or killed an animal or I don't know what to think. I find my car badly parked around the corner and check it all over. There's no blood on the car, no dents. I didn't hit anyone. I'm relieved. I get into the car to drive back to my street and find a wad of tissues with dried blood all over it. I spend the day calling people I had seen at the party to find out what time I had gone home. Everyone tells me I seemed fine when I left the party and that I left pretty early.

"I stop calling people. I spend all that Sunday retracing the drive from my place to Bel Air where the party was. Then I'd drive home slowly looking for anything, any clue. Then I'd drive back and come home a different route, thinking I might have driven another way.

"To this day I do not know what happened that night. I know that I never wanted to drive again. I even stopped driving for a long time. I moved back to New York so I could walk and take cabs, but that's not when I stopped drinking. That's when I stopped driving.

"Now I am sober. Ninety days sober. Ninety meetings in 90 days. And I am depressed. Everyone says to wait for the miracle. I'm waiting. I guess I've rambled enough. Thanks for listening."

I hear applause, but speaking to the AA group is almost like being in a black out.

Chapter 41

My Dad Could Pick Them

I rarely hear from my dad. I check in with him periodically and listen to stories about Off-Track Betting. He is a very funny man and he tells a good story.

In time Betty forgives him and he forgives her and they get back together. The kids, Sandy and Vicki, graduate from Lincoln High School and get on with their lives. Betty works from home while my dad goes into the city every day to OTB where he is president of the union. Dad is still a bookie, in a way, but it's legal now.

Betty is the real bookie. She is the middle woman in an intricate betting scheme. Betty sits at home, the phone rings, and it's the actual bettor who says.

"Put 10-thousand on the Giants. This is Gus."

Betty immediately hangs up and dials another number and says.

"Ten thousand. Giants."

Then someone else calls Gus. Probably some other happy homemaker. I don't know exactly how many phone calls it takes to place one bet, but it is exceptionally difficult to trace. Every few months, Betty calls the phone company and reports harassment calls, and gets a new unlisted phone number to confuse the issue a little more.

Finally, Betty and Dad put together enough money to buy a condo in a building facing the Boardwalk, facing the sea on Brighton First Street. Betty struggles long and hard to get my dad out of the family tenement on Fourth Street. Now that she has won her battle, it turns out he loves having a semi-view of the ocean from a concrete balcony and living the long three blocks from the rest of his family. His younger brother moved to Ocean Parkway years before. They never travel far from one another even through all the animosity among my dad, his dad, my uncle and my aunt.

Sandy, my half-brother, is a good person. Good in school, good at sports, and when he graduates he marries a pretty Jewish girl and moves to New Jersey. I feel closer to him in many ways than to other family members—on Dad's side, anyway. He commutes to the city every day to work with our dad at OTB. He has a quasi-normal life, two sons, and a love of acting.

Vicki, my half-sister, who has been verbally abused by the entire family since birth, dates boys who abuse her, and then marries one or two who continue the abuse. She is a sweetheart, but her pain is her motivation. She has three children, two boys and a girl. I wish I may I wish I might know her better, but I don't.

When my father's death comes in the middle of the night, he is 84-years-old and still the president of OTB.

Betty describes his last night to me over the phone on January 4, 1999.

"Sharon, honey, he woke me up in the middle of the night hollering for his pills. I told him to get them himself. He was always yelling for something. I didn't realize what was going on.

"And that's how I found him in the morning. He was half on the couch and half on the floor holding that damn bottle. There were pills all over the place. If I'd have got up and found his pills for him, he might be alive. I miss him so much now."

"It's not your fault, Betty. How could you have known?"

"I tore up your dad's will and the lawyer destroyed the office copies, too. There was nothing much in it anyway. You'll have to sign a waiver. Is that okay?" Betty tells me all this through her tears.

I suddenly realize she's talking about the same lawyer who arranged my Mexican divorce. Good friend of the family.

The funeral details I get from my brother Sandy.

What does it matter anyway about the will? He is gone. He is gone and he was never *there*. I loved my father. I have an album filled with 8x10 glossies of him. He loved being photographed, especially with celebrities. He hated that I would never ask any of the few well-known people I met over the years to pose for a picture to send to him.

Chapter 42

Charles Alton Pfahl III

New York 1993

Almost two years into my sobriety and three years into my return to New York, Charles, the artist I knew as Chuck, so long ago, calls me. He tells me that since he left everything he owned when he left the country in the 80s, he also got rid of his childhood nickname and finally became himself. Charles Alton Pfahl III. He's in from one of his journeys abroad. I had hoped I'd never see him again, but opportunities to make amends don't come along that often. I want to apologize and take responsibility for the part I played in ruining our lives together in the 70s. I'm on a roll, so when he asks me to have dinner with him, I say yes. I am very nervous about seeing him again.

We agree to meet at Teacher's Restaurant on Broadway. The last time we were at that restaurant, we both got drunk and went back to my apartment on 85th Street and made love, the week before he got married.

I open the door at Teachers and see Charles sitting alone at a table in the center of the crowded side room. He is drinking a beer and his face is puffy and red. I am afraid and mumble the serenity prayer under my breath as I walk around the low wooden barrier to where he sits.

He stands up. He looks happy to see me. It's winter again. And I smile.

He smiles that beautiful smile.

"I didn't think you'd come."

"I didn't want to—at first—but now that I see you, I'm glad I changed my mind. How are you? How long has it been?"

"Too long."

After our dinner, Charles is very drunk. He walks me across Broadway to the bus stop and waits there until the uptown 104 comes. I feel closer to him tonight than I ever have. He strokes my shoulder and a familiar tingle runs through my body and I take a deep breath. On my bus ride uptown, I fantasize about how nice it could be if Charles would stop drinking and doing drugs. I realize that I have never really stopped loving him. At home my phone is already ringing when I walk in.

It's Charles. He wants to go to an AA meeting.

"I will pass your building at 11:30 tomorrow morning," I tell him. "If you're there, you are more than welcome to go with me. If you're not there, I'll go anyway."

I know the odds are not in my favor that he will be waiting for me on the corner in the morning. But I pray for guidance and I pray that he is ready to stop the insanity in his life, too.

Morning comes quickly. I read for a while, shower, drink as much coffee as I can get into my body and head downtown. I'm still out of work and focusing on recovery. I am also going more deeply into debt.

All the way from 89th Street I can see Charles standing in the cold outside Jack Paramore's building on 81st. His home away from no home. I wave, but he doesn't see me yet. I am grateful that he's going to a meeting with me. I hope I have learned not to get my hopes up, though, regarding alcoholics.

"Charles!"

He walks toward me on that late November day. A kiss and we are on our way to AA.

I rattle on about not much of anything until we reach the Y on 63rd Street. I make numerous attempts to reassure him, but I don't think he registers even half of what I am saying.

"It is a large meeting. Charles, you don't have to say or do anything. These people love to talk. Mostly actors and musicians, performers. We can both just listen and afterwards we'll go to lunch with some friends."

He agrees to whatever I say and I am astonished.

Charles seems slightly nervous and still high on something. His ordinarily beautiful blue eyes are just tiny slits. Only pinpoint pupils in there when he smiles. But he smiles and my heart skips a beat. Just like the old days.

It turns out to be a good meeting. Charles pays attention to the speaker, shakes hands afterwards with my friends Paul, Michael, Ursula, Laurie, Don and a few others I consider pillars of sobriety.

Charles isn't able to take it all in, but we trudge on with him hoping he'll be better at lunch. All goes well and we walk him home as a group.

The next day is Sunday and I stop at Jack's to retrieve Charles on my way to another Westside meeting. Charles sits in an overstuffed chair in Jack's den surrounded by his own paintings, paintings Jack has bought over the years. Brown paper shopping bags full of empty beer cans also surround him. He pops another open and drinks.

I feel actual physical pain seeing him like this. I'm sad and angry at the same time. Before I say anything I'll regret, I shake my head and blurt out.

"I'm going to a meeting. Call me if you'd ever like to go, again. Call whenever you like."

I cry all the way over to Columbus Avenue and 88th Street praying that Charles will get this, will get AA. If not now, then someday. He's lost somewhere I can't go back to and I feel sorry for him. I don't really understand why AA works for some and not others, but I pray for Charles.

That night I stay home and have dinner with Rick. Rick's a great cook and I love spending time with him, even though he has that one glass of gin every night. He's waiting for a call from someone he's just met, but when the phone rings, I nearly kill myself rushing to grab it before the answering machine picks up.

"Can I come over?"

It's Charles.

"You don't even know where I live."

"I can find it. I'll take a cab."

"Are you drunk?"

"Yes. I need to talk to you."

I think for a minute. Something new for me.

"Are you coming over now?"

I hear loud voices and party noises in the background.

"I'm with Jack and Valerie and a couple other old friends. See you soon? It's 10 o'clock. I should be there in less than 15 minutes. It's Valerie's husband's birthday, I think, or maybe it's tomorrow, but he's not here."

"Did you write down my address, Charles?"

"Yes."

I sit in the living room long after Rick gets his phone call and goes to bed. I am curled up on the loveseat reading all about Step 12 in the Big Book, where you help another alcoholic, but I still don't know what I am doing tonight.

At 10:30, I get fidgety and worry about what's happened to Charles.

At 11, Rick comes out of his room and tells me I should give up and go to bed, that Charles probably got talked into staying at the party.

"Whatever you do, do not go out looking for him. Okay?" he says.

Rick is protective of me, always has been. Just like a slightly older brother. I adore him, but he doesn't completely understand alcoholics. No one but another alcoholic can truly understand.

I wait as long as I can and then I call Jack's number.

"Hi, honey," Jack answers. "He left at 10, right after he talked to you."

It is 20 blocks straight up Broadway. Even if he'd walked, it would take 15 minutes. Tops.

A bit after midnight I finally hear a knock at the door.

"Where have you been? Are you all right?"

Charles looks at me like I'm insane. He's grinning.

"Of course, I'm all right. Why wouldn't I be all right?"

We sit on the loveseat in the living room and talk. I know he's completely out of it, but I plan to talk him sober and then send him back to Jack's in a cab. We talk forever. He tells me about Indonesia, Ireland, Italy—all the places he's lived and worked and loved since last I saw him—and about all the relationships with women, and there were several, and how badly they all ended.

I coax stories about his blackouts out of him to use as ammunition when he comes out of this one. It passes across my mind that all the places he lived start with the letter I.

Mid-sentence he stops talking and stares at me, then he looks around the apartment.

"Where am I?"

"You're at my place."

"How did I get here?"

"I was hoping you could tell me."

"What time is it?"

"Three."

He looks at me as if I'm lying. Then at his watch.

"I left Jack's right after we talked. What time did I get here?"

"About midnight. Charles. You have just come out of a blackout. Mid-sentence. We've been talking for hours."

Stunned, he asks shyly, "Did I say anything terrible? Did I tell you where I spent those two hours between 10 and midnight?"

I shake my head.

He looks around the apartment.
"This is nice."
He stares at me for a long time.
"Please take me to bed."

Chapter 43

Life's Terms

Charles dedicates himself to getting sober. Life on life's terms is not an easy concept to grasp, but he has AA support—and my support, as well. And he is very strong and ready for a new life.

A few days sober but still smoking pot, I take a chance.

"Do you know how distant you are when you're smoking?" I ask him.

He had never thought about it in that way. That is his last joint.

I temp for a while around the city, mostly at ABC, and then I take a fulltime job at Sony.

When Charles sells a couple of paintings, we use the money to move into an apartment atop a nine-story building on 71st Street. A tiny place. It is on the roof and it's just right for Charles and me. We have our patio and barbecue and all the comforts I haven't even thought about in years. We are next door to a church and the stained glass windows become part of our beautiful world. Charles devises an intricate lighting system that aims the beams on the windows. It's like living in a cathedral.

Charles begins to paint—for the first time since getting sober—and the paintings are even more magnificent. He always says he can paint anywhere and it's true. There's barely enough room for an easel in our miniature bedroom.

This time our love is without drugs and alcohol or rage. And I go to one or two or three meetings a day, waiting for a miracle. This sober life with Charles is a miracle and I am happy to be living it. He is the love of my life. All I ever wanted was to love and be loved. I have it all now. And a best friend who actually likes me. What could be better than that?

Chapter 44

Post-Party Depression

Not many things could drag me back to Los Angeles now. One of them is my devotion to Tom. I dream one night that he is happy, doing well. So I call him out of the blue and tell him what a wonderful dream I had. The other end of the phone goes silent for a long time.

"Tom, are you there? Tom?"

"I have cancer. Esophageal."

I am horrified and don't really know what to say first.

"Do you want me to come and help you? If you do, you'll have to ask me. But if you ask me, I'll come."

And after another long silence, he asks.

"Please come. I'm alone. You can have our tree house when I die, if you come and help me now."

"You're not dying, Tom."

"Maybe not, but I wish I'd been kinder to you when you were sick and in pain. I can't stand this—all this pain. I have never known this kind of pain."

I go to Los Angeles and when I see how sick Tom really is, I call Emma and his older sister and ask them to come to Los Angeles right now. Right now.

I help Tom write his will.

"I know I promised you our little tree house, but it's the only thing I have to leave Emma. Do you want my car?"

Tom dies in the living room of the little tree house we once owned together in Silver Lake—April 25, 1999. He is an old and also young 53 and doesn't get to see the new century and all its horror and for that I grieve and for that I am sometimes grateful. I suffer from Tom's death more than any other loss I've ever experienced. So far. Tom's death is dark and denied. He does not go gently. His sister and daughter, and the downstairs renter and I are with him when he goes wherever he goes.

His last words to me are, "I love you." I always wanted him to say that. We both cry at this late revelation. Then he said he couldn't see, that he was blind. And then he said, "Oh, my god!"

His death is ugly, horrific. Chemotherapy, radiation, transfusions, morphine. Tom always said he did not want to die in Los Angeles. But at least his sister takes his ashes home with her to England and scatters them across the Mersey, near a beach where they played as children.

I see him all the time in other people. On the street, at work, everywhere. I am always aware of his presence in the tree house and even in the gray Saab he left me. Poor Tom. I pray that he is somewhere light and bright and hopeful.

Chapter 45

All Over Town

Dr. Parikh calls me from Akron. I am sober and enjoying my second time around with Charles in New York. Parikh has been my mother's psychiatrist since Dr. Dove Roman retired years ago. I met him once and was not impressed, but he keeps her on track. After the initial hello, he says,

"Last night I ran into your mother at Lawson's, a convenience store here in Fairlawn. She was disoriented. Didn't know where she was, why she was there, who I was. She had driven there on her own."

"Thank you for letting me know, Dr. Parikh. I'll call her and visit as soon as I can get a flight."

"Make your arrangements fast."

Click.

Why didn't that doctor watch her more closely? She has been his patient for 20 years, his and Dr. Roman's. I don't think much of him as a psychiatrist, that's for sure. But then I never bothered to talk to him before. No need to, I thought. Why am I so surprised by what is happening—that denial is catching up with me?

I dial my mother's number. It rings a long, long time as usual. She doesn't hurry for anything, especially an intruder, a telephone intruder.

"Hello?"

"Mother, it's me."

"Oh, is it?"

"Yes, how are you?"

"Fine."

"What are you doing?"

"Watching TV and drinking Kool-Aid. You know I can't get those cats to come out of hiding."

"Is it all right if I come to see you at the end of the week?"

"What day is this?"

"Wednesday."

"Did you lose your job?"

"No, I didn't lose my job. I love you, Mother."

"Do you?"
"See you soon."
Click.

She sounds fine except I know she doesn't have cats, or even a cat.

I take a Continental flight into Cleveland Hopkins Airport where I rent a car and drive to Akron, about 30 minutes away. I call my mother to remind her I'm on my way. When I get to her house on Barrington Road, she doesn't come to the door. I knock, ring, pound, kick. Finally I go next door to the neighbors' house to see if they know what's going on. They don't say much but look at me in an eerie way. I call my mother from their house. This time she answers.

"Hello?"

"Mother, it's me. I'm next door at your neighbors' house. Will you let me in, please?"

"What are you doing there?"

When I finally get inside the house, I am so sad. She sits in her La-Z-Boy recliner and stares at me. The Kool-Aid she spilled looks like blood on her plush light-colored wall-to-wall carpet.

Her right ankle is swollen and when I ask about it, she can't remember how it happened. I make a mental note to stay calm and take her to the doctor first thing in the morning.

I need to get her ready for bed. First I help her into the shower stall and turn on the water. She screams when I walk away because she is facing the shower wall and forgets where she is. She doesn't know what a shower is. I turn off the water and dry her off. She is almost hysterical. After she has her pajamas on and is in bed I go downstairs.

There are dishes full of cat food all over the house. And litter boxes that have never been used but are overflowing with clean litter.

I yell up to her.

"Mother, I don't think any cats live here."

She laughs out loud.

"Then who eats all the food?"

I go back upstairs and kiss her goodnight.

It is impossible for me to fall asleep in my old bedroom, Darryl's old bedroom. It is dark and I realize I could be anywhere. Anywhere.

The Bridge

As I go in and out of sleep, I remember a Pat somebody or other and the High Level Bridge in downtown Akron. He is someone I haven't thought of in years.

But he remains a permanent black-and-white slide lodged in a dark corner of my brain. Frozen there since I was five. My mother's condition forces the slide to drop in front of my eyes and makes me remember a part of my special day with this Pat guy.

My mother and I—and that man Pat—are together on the bridge.

I wear a brand new red winter coat over my brown checked dress with the white embroidered collar. I'm dressed up. My black patent-leather shoes shine and my ankle socks are snowy white with just a tiny bit of lace, but they are not enough to keep me warm on this wintry day. My legs are cold. My hands are cold.

Mommy is in a hurry to get somewhere. Somewhere downtown. The courthouse maybe. Somewhere important. I can tell she doesn't want to take me wherever she's going today. She takes me to bars and shopping and parties, but this is different. She dressed me up to go with her and is having second thoughts. Thoughts that worry her. Anger her.

She's a little bit ahead of me. He is behind me. I walk as fast as I can to keep up with her. My arms are stretched as far as they can be. She holds one hand; Pat holds the other. I try to stay close to her, but I am afraid I will be ripped apart.

In the middle of the bridge, they stop suddenly. My mommy has no face. Pat has no face. It's snowing now and soft white flakes blur my vision. The wind howls like Grandpa's dogs when they hear a police car siren.

"Kate, I'll take care of her." Pat whispers across the wind to Mommy. "You go on ahead and do what you have to do. I'll meet you at that bar on Main Street. Whitelaw's. You and Bob."

I twist my hand from his and turn to her.

"I don't want to go with him, Mommy."

She drops my hand. The wind is a sword cutting through my heart as I watch her run away from me toward downtown and into the past. She wears a scarf to cover her beautiful red hair and sunglasses to cover her swollen eyes. Maybe it isn't even her.

She doesn't look back.

Pat picks me up and pulls me close to him. He wears a blue wool navy coat with big buttons and he's smiling. His eyes are blue and there are tiny holes in his face. A few deep scars. His breath smells of morning whisky and Lucky Strikes. He has the end of a cigarette in his mouth now and I'm afraid it will touch me. Burn my face. I put my hands on his chest and push away from him. I turn my head away from his smell.

He keeps rubbing my ice-cold legs as we turn to go in the other direction. Away from downtown. Away from her.

He rubs my freezing legs with one rough hand while he puts the other up under my favorite dress.

Now I have no face. The sleeve of my coat is stark against the darkening sky and I crawl into my head so I can watch myself in Pat's arms as he walks away with me.

Pat is Bob's friend. His drinking buddy from the Navy.

Pat has rooms in an old boarding house. The floors are covered with cracked, faded yellow linoleum. It's as cold inside as out. He lives near downtown where no one else I know lives.

I try to make myself remember something nice. A week ago, I got an envelope in the mail with my name on it from Daddy. I have the letter in my patent-leather pocket book right now; I keep it with the white hanky with the "S" on it and the pink Canada Mint my grandma gave me last Sunday before she left for church.

I sit on the cold floor and open my pocket book. I pull out a picture. It's Daddy, just his handsome head and shoulders. He is smiling. His teeth are white. He wrote across his right shoulder on the sort of fuzzy black-and-white picture, *"Sweetheart, no matter what happens... never lose your sense of humor. Love, Daddy."*

Mommy says he's an idiot to write something like that to a five-year-old.

I keep seeing my mommy's face.

In the middle of that bridge, my mommy lets go of my hand. The sky is gray.

When she lets go of my hand, I feel like she's giving me away.

Back to Real Time

I am older, so much older now, yet this image remains a black-and-white slide in a distant corner of my head.

And I finally fall asleep in the bedroom across the hall from my mother's room. I drift off thinking I must remember to tell Dr. Dan about this childhood memory.

Tomorrow is going to be a difficult day.

Chapter 46

Jewels

My mother lives at Jewel Care in Mount Washington, just two blocks from where Darryl bought his house in a mountainous corner of Los Angeles. He found the place when he was jogging one day. It is a godsend—a psychiatric board and care with just five women in residence. Jewel runs the home and Loretta cooks and cleans. Annie lives there, too, and she is not demented at all and has her own room. Annie is the best friend my mother has ever had. Mother's roommate, Virginia, thinks she's the Virgin Mary and my mother goes along with it. The other two ladies share a separate larger bedroom and bath.

    Mother spends weekends—days only—with just Charles and me usually, but this weekend he and I are taking her to Escondido to celebrate an early Christmas with Darryl and his wife Diane. Darryl married just the right person for him and I am so happy for them. They are angels.

    The drive is uneventful and we get there too early. We should have stopped for lunch, but we didn't. On arrival, Mother is not in a good mood and can't or won't participate in what is going on. She eats lots of chocolate candy and drinks a diet Coke. Diane and Darryl prepare a delicious meal for all of us, but Mother leaves the table early. She isn't feeling so great; her stomach is bothering her. So she goes to bed even before we have a chance to give her her Christmas gifts.

    She dies sometime between midnight and six a.m. I check on her at seven in the morning and she is not breathing. She is ice cold. I touch her hand, her face, and watch her for a minute or two. She is not breathing. I notice an overturned glass on the floor and realize that during the night she must have reached for her glass of water and spilled it all over her Anguilla nightshirt, so she has taken it off and is wearing only gray underpants and a gray tank top. The tank top reads, "Wicked." It is a Walt Disney promotion tank top. She is lying on her right side with her right arm under her head. She wears the Seiko watch that Darryl bought her a few years ago and that Charles had the battery changed in yesterday. She wears the ring she had bought from Aunt Pat, so many years ago, and a double pearl ring I gave her last year or the year before. The double pearl ring was her mother's, but she didn't know that.

And now she is dead. Her eyes are slightly open. I cover her with a blanket and walk out to the kitchen where Darryl and Charles are having coffee.

"I think Mother is dead."

At first they laugh. They think I'm kidding.

Darryl goes to the room and returns quickly.

"She is dead."

I wait with her body while Darryl makes the proper calls. 911, fire department, police. I don't know how many calls he has to make.

I kiss her cheek and talk to her.

"I love you, Mother."

The night before her death, she was tired. During the night, when I checked on her, she was lying in bed awake and said she still had indigestion.

"It's because you're tired from the long drive, and you have that ulcer too." I asked her to describe the pain. She said it burned her. She asked for her Tums and I gave her two of them. I fluffed her pillows, put a warm blanket over her. We talked about all the chocolate she had eaten, how she had this ulcer for a long time and that she always forgot about the pain because of her dementia so that the pain surprised her every time it came.

"Sharon, I can't sleep."

I told her to take a deep breath and to try to sleep and that tomorrow everything would be all right.

A couple of hours later she came out and went into the bathroom. I met her in the hallway and asked how she was feeling. She said the pain was gone, but that she felt very weak. I walked her to the bedroom, tucked her in and left her for the night. She asked me to lie down with her for a while, but I kissed her again and said, "Just get some rest. You'll be better in the morning, you'll see."

Well, it is morning now and she is dead. And she never even got to open her gifts.

Epilogue

I bought that little Los Angeles tree house twice: the first time in 1981 when Tom and I saw an ad in The L.A. Weekly. The owner was the daughter of a Swedish man who built it back in the early 1930s. She had lived there all her life. It was only a three-owner house.

When Tom died, the house was in foreclosure, but he wanted Emma to have something from him. I had a job where I made enough money to qualify for a loan, and Charles and I borrowed the rest of the money to get it out of foreclosure and to put a down payment on it. When we got the loan, we were able to give Emma some money, so that she did, in essence, get an inheritance from her father, and she did not have to live with a foreclosure hanging over her head for the rest of her life. Tom loved Emma very much. I loved her, too. And Charles and I had a wonderful tree house to live in.

Tom is dead and his ashes float in the Mersey.

Mother is wherever mothers go.

Darryl and Diane still live in Escondido and they are doing very well.

There was no reason for us to live in Los Angeles any longer, so Charles and I sold the Silver Lake tree house.

Wish us luck.

A friend told me that there's a tomb in the Templar's church in London and on it is written, "Repaired and Beautified." That's how I think of my mother.

The End

Sharon van Ivan currently lives in Albuquerque, New Mexico, with her two cats, The Duke and Earl.

The artist Charles Pfahl, who was the love of her life, died October 4, 2013.

She is in the process of learning all over again the true meaning of living one day at a time.

Published by Cygnet Press
©2014, Sharon van Ivan/Cygnet Press
P.O. Box 3941
Albuquerque, NM 87190
www.cygnetpress.com
info@cygnetpress.com
ISBN-10: 0983349843
ISBN-13: 978-0-9833498-4-6
LCCN: 2014939591

The image on both covers, "Juggle and Hide," is used by permission of the artist and copyrighted by Charles Pfahl©.

Cover images photographed by Pat Berrett.

Design and layout by Timothy B. Anderson/Cygnet Press

Permission is granted to reviewers to print selected copy as examples. Reviewers are requested to send copies of reviews.

www.ingramcontent.com/pod-product-compliance
Lightning Source LLC
Chambersburg PA
CBHW020648300426
44112CB00007B/286